HIT IT HARD!

The Modern Fundamentals of Power Golf

Mike Dunaway and
John Andrisani

ILLUSTRATIONS BY KEN LEWIS

SIMON & SCHUSTER
New York London Toronto Sydney Tokyo Singapore

Simon & Schuster
Simon & Schuster Building
Rockefeller Center
1230 Avenue of the Americas
New York, New York 10020

Designed by Irving Perkins Associates
Manufactured in the United States of America

10 9 8 7 6 5 4 3 2 1

Library of Congress Cataloging in Publication Data

Dunaway, Mike.
Hit it hard! : the modern fundamentals of power golf / Mike Dunaway and John Andrisani ; illustrations by Ken Lewis.
p. cm.
1. Golf. I. Andrisani, John. II. Title.
GV965.D76 1992
796.352—dc20 91-34260
CIP

ISBN: 0-671-73490-3

I would like to dedicate this book to all those people who helped me out when I really needed it:

Mike Austin
Dorothy Dunaway
Debbie Moore
Mel Simon
John Brim
Charlie Bell
Emmitt Munley
John Coleman
Hiroshi Takahama
Dick Helmstetter

CONTENTS

FOREWORD

In August 1986, at the Inverness Country Club, in Toledo, Ohio, site of the PGA Championship that year, I was scheduled to give a shotmaking exhibition with Byron Nelson. The long-game portion of the exhibition was not going to be given by Greg Norman or Davis Love or Fred Couples—but by Mike Dunaway of Arkansas.

I had heard the name, Mike Dunaway, and knew about his reputation for hitting long drives, but I had never actually seen him swing. In fact, to be honest, before he gave the exhibition, I thought he was just going to be another "big knocker" with an unorthodox swing, who depended on sheer brute strength to power the golf ball. Was I in for a surprise!

From the moment Dunaway took his first powerful swipe at the ball, I knew he was a special breed with a truly great golf swing. Ball after ball zoomed off the clubface and flew dead-straight for over 320 yards before hitting the fairway.

What's so extraordinary about Dunaway is that he generates world-record clubhead speed, yet makes hitting the ball look effortless. That's because the foundation for his mechanically flawless swing is a set of "address fundamentals" which I adhere to myself and stress in the articles I write for *Golf Magazine.* Moreover, Dunaway works the joints and muscles of his body so efficiently that he repeatedly arrives in the classic swing positions and maintains perfect balance during the entire motion. And good balance just so happens to be the number one prerequisite to great tempo, timing, and power.

Ever since that day of the shotmaking exhibition at Inverness, I've kept tabs on Mike. Frankly, it came as no shock to me that, in 1989, he took up a challenge to drive a golf ball across the Arkansas River, and won; his drive flew 330 yards before touching down on the sandy shore way over yonder. I wasn't surprised either to find out that Dunaway won the 1990 Super Long Drive Contest in Japan.

I'm happy that Dunaway has finally put his secrets down on paper; we can all learn a lot from him about power golf.

KEN VENTURI

WRITER'S COMMENTARY

I'll never forget how I met Mike Dunaway. I was sitting in my office at *Golf Magazine* in New York when the telephone rang. On the other end was a young-sounding man with a country-boy accent. His name was Mike Dunaway. He claimed he was the longest hitter in the world, and he was willing to prove it.

Because of my position at *Golf* (senior editor: instruction), I regularly receive about a hundred calls per week, a dozen of which come from "quacks" who insist they've discovered some hidden swing tip in an old book they found in their attic, invented a swing gadget that is guaranteed to groove a perfect putting stroke, or dare I say, discovered *the secret* to the swing.

I'm always amused most by those callers who claim to have found the ultimate swing secret, because for some reason when they're on the line, I drift off into a state of mental peace conjuring up wonderful images of Christopher Columbus arriving on the shores of a strange undiscovered land, or of an ancient tomb filled with precious gold relics and bottles of elixir being discovered in an Egyptian pyramid. Maybe this escape is my defense mechanism in dealing with quacks, or maybe hearing the word "secret" stirs up such a feeling of hope that a sense of euphoria comes over me. I'm not really sure.

A big part of my job at *Golf* is to screen golf nuts, just in case somebody truly has discovered the secret to a perfect swing. So, in my usual manner of protocol, I politely asked: "Mr. Dunaway, just how do you intend to prove that you are, indeed, the world's longest hitter of a golf ball?" Dunaway's reply: "I'll challenge anyone to outhit me for

$10,000, winner take all," he calmly said, with the confident air of Mike Tyson. "Okay," I said, immediately sensing that, if nothing else, this could be a great story for *Golf* to run in an upcoming issue.

George Peper, the editor-in-chief of *Golf Magazine,* agreed with me about the potential marquee sales value of such a story. "We can't lose, Andrisani, let's check him out," he said. We did just that, at the 1985 "Golf Week" we hosted at the Sawgrass Resort in Florida for our advertisers.

One morning, a gallery of editorial and advertising guests gathered around the tee of the Sawgrass Resort's driving range, when along came that burly country boy I had spoken to on the telephone a month earlier. As he moseyed on over to the tee in typical southern fashion, I thought to myself, "Let the show begin."

I'll never forget the feeling of shock that ran through my body when I saw him swing at around 150 mph and send the ball sailing 300 yards, clear across the driving range into a resident's yard. In less than two seconds—the time it takes him to swing—he had proved to me, and the goggle-eyed group of spectators too, that he was for real. All present agreed that Dunaway had the most technically sound, graceful-looking, powerful golf swing that they had ever seen anyone employ.

Long before the show was over, Peper and I agreed that we would put Dunaway on the cover of our August issue with the "teaser" $10,000 SAYS YOU CAN'T OUTHIT ME in bold print. We also agreed that we should play with Dunaway the next day to see how he performed in a "real" golf situation.

On the golf course, Dunaway was even more awesome. Now, Peper and I are not short off the tee; we each hit an average drive about 250 yards, which is pretty much pro standard. Well, I'll tell you, this quiet boy from the Arkansas woods made us feel like a pair of driving wimps!

On every single par four and par five, Dunaway outhit us by between 75 and 100 yards. On one hole, a dogleg par five of 587 yards, Peper and I each boomed a drive and then a fairway wood over water, to reach the green in two shots. Tour pros don't even do that all of the time; but still, Dunaway burst our bubble. He reached the hole in two with a drive and—a pitching wedge!

At a cocktail party that evening, Greg Norman, our guest speaker (who didn't know Dunaway was attending, but who, we later found out, had once seen Mike hit balls at a tournament in Japan), walked over to Dunaway, put his arm around him, and said, "This man is the longest driver in the world." When you consider that "The Great White Shark" was regarded as the world's longest tour professional, that was quite an endorsement—not that we needed one. (In 1991, John Daly, the tour's longest driver, who caused a sensation at the PGA Championship when he launched rocket drive after rocket drive on his way to victory, told the press in a post-tournament interview that Dunaway was one man who could outhit him.)

The August 1985 issue of *Golf Magazine* turned out to be an all-time best seller. What's more, Dunaway's $10,000 challenge prompted a cable television station to run a weekly show called *Tee It Up*. On that show, Dunaway challenged and beat fifteen big hitters, including touring golf professional Fred Couples and Lawrence Taylor of the New York Giants.

Accolades such as these (highlighted by Dunaway's 1990 victory in the World Super Long Drive Contest), plus the fact that his tips have helped me gain twenty yards on my drives, are what made me want to collaborate on *Hit It Hard! The Modern Fundamentals of Power Golf*.

In this book, Dunaway shares his power-driving secrets and presents, too, through clear technical language and lucid illustrations, easy-to-follow instruction on everything from power-iron play to using the power of the mind to picking the right driver.

In reading *Hit It Hard,* pay closest attention to Dunaway's unique setup position, hip coil on the backswing, and arm-slinging action on the downswing. Then learn to feel and groove the entire swing motion through drillwork.

One last thing: When you call me at *Golf Magazine* to say you've discovered the secret, be sure to mention that Dunaway taught you. Then I'll know you're no quack.

JOHN ANDRISANI

INTRODUCTION

When I was nine years old, I received a telephone call from a member of the Conway Country Club in Conway, Arkansas, asking me to play in their annual junior golf tournament. I entered the tournament—well, a sort of tournament, anyway. There was only one other golfer competing in the nine- and ten-year-old division: Gumpy Thompson. Gumpy shot 54 and I scored 36—for four holes!

When I look back at it now, that one small junior event played a big role in shaping my golf destiny. Another major event, a football game, also steered me toward a career in golf.

Growing up, I was blessed with natural athletic skills and attended college on a football scholarship. However, on the first play of my junior year, I sustained a back injury that ended my future in football. From that day forward, I began to obsessively search for the secret to hitting the ball hard.

In my quest to unravel the mysteries of the golf swing and discover the true mechanical keys to effortless power, I made endless trips to what I like to call the *mumble shed.* The mumble shed is the place in my mind where I would go when the "wheels came off" and I was feeling frustrated. There, I used to talk to myself; and after a few minutes I would always come to the same conclusion: *The search for the perfect swing takes countless hours of trial and error, analysis and reanalysis, hard work and determination.*

In 1977, I met a teacher, Mike Austin, who is in the *Guinness Book of World Records* for hitting the longest drive during a round of golf—515 yards! Austin used his knowledge of motion and human anatomy to teach me the most efficient way to swing a golf club. In my opinion, Mike Austin's methods are 20 years ahead of any current teaching. His background in kineseology, engineering, psychology, medicine, and professional golf enables him to remove the veil of mystery that surrounds the golf swing. I will be sharing several aspects of what I call Austinology in this book. Nobody knows more about the golf swing than Mike Austin.

From the time I first stepped on the lesson tee with Austin, I started making fewer trips to the mumble shed. Eventually everything started to click. However, it wasn't until 1990, the year I won the World Super Long Drive Contest in Japan, that I was convinced that I had mastered a power technique that any golfer could easily clone. It was then that I phoned John Andrisani, the senior editor of instruction at *Golf Magazine,* and asked him if he would collaborate with me on *Hit It Hard! The Modern Fundamentals of Power Golf.*

Even though I was absolutely sure that the method of swinging I learned from Austin was easier to repeat than any other technique I had been introduced to or had read about in instruction books, during the writing of *Hit It Hard!,* a number of questions came to mind: "Do these words clearly and accurately describe this movement?" "Is this illustration effective?" "Am I trying to impress the reader with my knowledge, instead of helping him?"

Our common goal in writing this book was to provide simple applicable instruction that would benefit all levels of golfers. Hopefully, *Hit It Hard!* will help you gain a little extra distance and control off the tee and make a vital difference to your overall performance on the golf course—which will go a long way toward keeping you out of the mumble shed.

MIKE DUNAWAY

HIT IT HARD!

1

THE POWER SETUP

How you address the ball determines the quality of your driving

Whatever one does in life, success is always dictated by the five Ps: *Proper Planning Prevents Poor Performance.* In golf, proper planning means building a solid foundation or "setup" by perfecting, through hard, dedicated practice, the elements of grip, ball position, alignment, posture, and stance.

I learned long ago that if only one of these five setup elements is incorrect, a compensation must be made during the swing. Otherwise, the club cannot be swung on the correct path and plane, and at a sufficient speed, to return it squarely to the ball and make a powerful hit at impact.

Having said that, if your ultimate golf goal is to become a consistently long and accurate driver of the ball, then you must first build a concrete foundation that requires no compensatory movements. The best starting point in achieving this goal is to learn how to put your hands on the club properly.

In a golf swing, power is created by winding the body on the backswing. And when the body unwinds—or rather, springs back quickly—that created stored power is transferred from the body to the arms, then through the hands to the clubhead. Because a powerful swing is thus dependent on the evenly timed, perfectly sequential motion of the entire body, it's crucial to control the club *through* the hands, not with them.

From the time I trigger my swing, my hands merely go along for the ride. Basically, the powerful coiling action of my body carries my hands up to the top of my swing. The slinging action of my arms, made more powerful by centrifugal force acting on them, thrusts them down and through during the second half of my swing, called simply the *downswing.* Silencing the hands—hitting *through* them—is what prevents me from manipulating the club, which is precisely why I consistently deliver the clubface squarely into the ball and hit drives on a dead-straight, bulletlike trajectory.

I don't want to give the impression that the hands play no key role in my swing, because that's not true at all. Logically, since my hands are my only connection to the club, I'm sure they play a more important role than even I imagine. However, I certainly can guarantee to you that I don't consciously whip the club into the ball at record speed with my hands. No human being could consciously direct the hands during the downswing. The motion is flowing too fast for that. While the backswing takes one and one-half seconds, the downswing takes less than two-fifths of a second. Therefore, by the time the hands reach the hit zone, at waist level on the downswing, they are already on a mission that cannot be redirected by the conscious mind.

For the swing (but particularly the downward movement) to work essentially on "automatic pilot," there has to be an even compromise between underactive and overactive hands. Basically, if you *choke* the grip, you totally *deaden* the hands and ultimately lose power on your drives. If you grip too *lightly,* you give the hands too much *life* and ultimately lose accuracy.

Swing faults traced to a bad grip become ingrained over years of playing. Therefore, a correct grip is, frankly, not going to instantly allow a player to iron out those faults and suddenly hit the ball long and straight. Nevertheless, if a golfer sacrifices some playing hours for some practice hours and works diligently on grooving a good grip, I honestly think, with time, he will correct some serious swing flaws that previously prevented him from increasing his individual power quotient. What's more, a novice at golf will learn to employ a power swing more quickly if he builds a good grip from the beginning.

Unlike many amateurs who consider the grip the "caboose" of the swing, I consider it the "engine," for it allows me to:

- Sole the clubface dead-square to my target as I set up to swing.
- Direct the clubhead on the correct plane and arc as established at address.
- Securely hold the club's handle and thus control it at critical points in the swing, particularly at the top, when the swinging weight of the club puts pressure on the hands and wrists, and also during the moment of impact, when very powerful forces are exerted on the golf club.
- Swing with sound tempo, timing, and rhythm.
- Transmit the power generated by the body to the head of the club, through the arms, then through the hands.
- Return the club squarely to the ball at tremendous speed as you relax the muscles you contracted in the backswing.

The type of grip you play with is a personal preference, but the basic keys for positioning the hands correctly on the handle of the club always apply.

To understand the fundamental principles that govern how the left and right hands should be placed on the club and how you should stand to the ball, pretend that your driver is soled on the ground (dead-square to a teed-up ball) and you are standing next to it, ready to take a lesson on the grip and the setup. Let me start by explaining the vital principles that dictate how the hands should be placed on the club.

THE LEFT-HAND GRIP

To program maximum comfort and control into your swing, allow the club's handle or grip-end to rest diagonally across the base of the fingers and only partially in the palm, with the end of it resting under the muscle pad of the hand's heel. (When the club is held mainly in the palm you lose the ability to control the clubface, which often results in a slice shot.)

When assuming the left-hand grip, let the club rest diagonally across the fingers and only partially in the palm.

Lay the left thumb almost straight down the shaft to ensure good control of the club.

To further program control and security into your grip, permit your thumb to lay pretty much straight down the shaft as far as is comfortably possible.

Next, check that the back portion of your hand faces the target (is *square* to it), and that between two and two and one-half knuckles appear as you look down. These two checks, particularly, verify that your left hand is set on the club correctly—in the ideal position to lead the club into the ball and keep its face square at impact when powerful forces are acting on it.

THE RIGHT-HAND GRIP

Let the club's handle lie predominantly in the roots of your fingers to ensure that the right hand is sensitive enough to control the acceleration through the ball. Now,

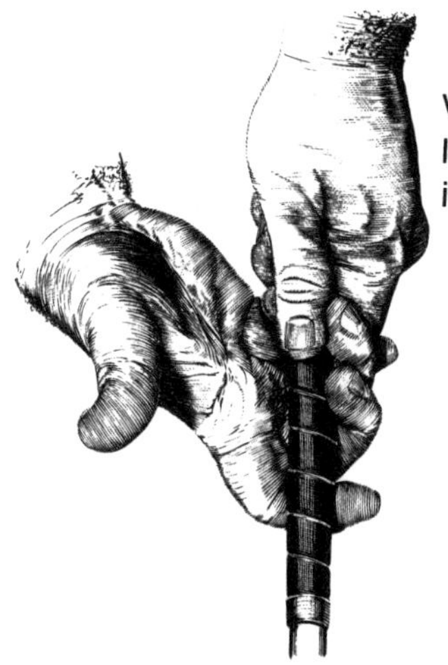

When gripping with the right hand, let the club's handle lie predominantly in your fingers.

A good grip sees the hands wedded together and the palms parallel to each other.

close your right hand so that its pad covers your left thumb, its palm faces your left one, and its thumb rides comfortably just to the target side of the top of the shaft. (For reasons of personal feel, I don't allow my right thumb and forefinger to touch when I grip the club. However, touching might help some of you with smaller fingers than mine hold the club more securely.)

You have just learned golf's most *basic* hold—the *ten-finger* or *baseball* grip. To assume the *interlock* grip, simply twine the right pinky between the first and middle fingers of your left hand. The *overlap* grip that I employ (as do the majority of top tour pros) involves laying the right pinky over the top of the left forefinger.

At different times during my long-drive career, I've experimented with all three of these grips. However, I'm through toying, and I now stick to the overlap hold for two reasons:

Placing the right pinky atop the left forefinger helps unify the hands.

1. It gives me such an ultimate sense of unity and feel in my hands that once the clubhead is set squarely on the ball, I never *milk* the grip (squeeze the handle and let go). Therefore, I never run the risk of moving it out of position—misaligning it to the target—before a swing.
2. It provides such a strong sense of security in my palms and wrists that I feel I can swing at maximum speed and still be in full control of the club. (Conversely, both the full-finger and the interlock grips give me such a loose feeling in my hands that I swing more slowly because I fear the clubhead might not finish square to the ball. However, even if it does finish "square," I lose clubhead speed and, therefore, vital distance off the tee.)

THE SETUP

Many club-level golfers who obsessively seek more distance on their drives take the setup for granted. That's very unfortunate, because to a great extent, ball position, posture, stance, and alignment of both the club and body (to the target) largely determine the type of swing a player makes—good or bad!

I realize that practicing the setup is not the most exciting thing in the world, yet if you know that mastering this seemingly insignificant part of the swing is highly critical to reaching your full power potential, then maybe somehow you can convince yourself that it's fun.

I, too, was once lackadaisical about learning the address, but eventually I got sick and tired of hitting the ball "long and wrong," so I consulted Mike Austin. Austin explained that by repeating the exact same pre-swing routine every time he set up to the ball, he prepared his subconscious mind for the best possible repetition of the intended swing. Once I understood that, I stopped stubbornly doing things my way and decided to mimic the basic way he and top-notch PGA tour players walk up to the ball and jockey themselves into a proper setup.

The best possible way for you to familiarize yourself with the critical elements of the setup and feel them, too, is to go through the steps of my "address rehearsal" with me, starting from when I stand behind the ball and look down the fairway.

MY STEP-BY-STEP PRE-SWING ROUTINE

Step One

To help me determine a target, I look intently at the shape of the hole (straight, dogleg left, dogleg right), and take into consideration the lurking hazards and the position of the pin on the green. I pick a target area of fairway that, once hit, will leave me with the most strategically smart approach shot into the hole. The natural shape of my shot is pretty straight, so unless the hole doglegs sharply, I usually aim down the middle of the fairway.

Step Two

Once I pick a target, some 300 yards down the fairway, I turn it into a *pool* of water. Next, in my mind's eye, I see myself swinging powerfully, true to plan, and the ball flying into the air, then coming down splashing the water. I focus so hard on the pool that I'm oblivious to anything else going on around me.

Step Three

I usually make one practice swing to help me rehearse my power swing. Ideally, I want this practice swing to be an exact duplicate (in terms of speed and shape) of the good swing I have grooved on the driving range.

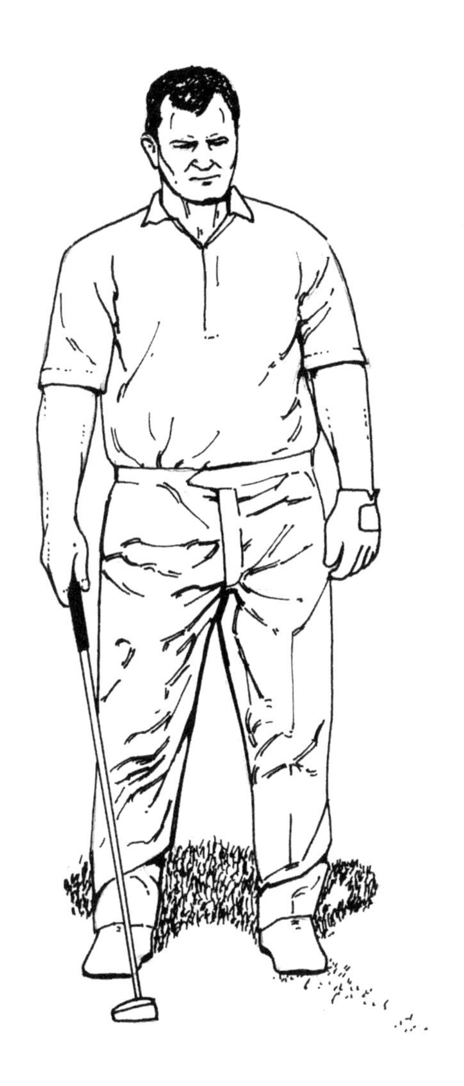

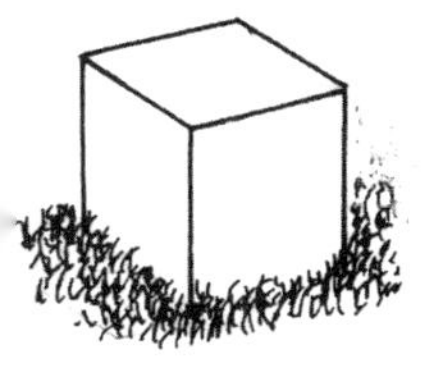

Standing behind the ball and looking down the fairway is crucial to mentally blocking out any hazards, and picking the ideal target area.

I'm not an advocate of practicing a slow version of your swing. To me that's like an actor rehearsing his lines without any emphasis on the words or phrases.

Step Four

This part of my setup is really three mini-steps combined into one, as I try to juggle my feet into a correct and comfortable position. I step to the ball, right foot first; lift

my left foot, moving it toward the target; lift my right foot, moving it away from the target.

Once my feet are flat on the ground and approximately shoulder-width apart (with my weight distributed evenly on the ball of each foot), I jockey myself around until I *feel* I've established a firm foundation and I *see* that both of my feet are angled out slightly—the left more than the right. Also, I check that the ball is opposite my left heel.

Fanning out my left foot about 20 degrees allows me to *clear* my left side more easily on the downswing, making

Jockeying your feet and body into position is crucial to establishing a comfortable and technically correct foundation for swinging.

room for my arms to whip the club freely into the ball. I fan my right foot out only about 10 degrees because I want it to enhance my hip turn, but to serve, also, as a brace to coil against.

Setting up with the ball forward promotes a clean hit on the upswing.

When teeing up to drive, about half of the ball should be above the top of the clubface.

I play the ball (which is teed up fairly high) slightly forward in my stance to encourage an upswing hit.

Step Five

Since the correct grip controls the position of the clubhead and the shoulders, I grip and regrip until I'm satisfied that the club is set squarely behind the ball, and that the shoulders—like the feet, knees, and hips—are parallel to the target line.

The parallel position of the feet, knees, hips, and shoulders allows me to arrive at the top of the backswing with the clubshaft parallel to the target line, and deliver the club down along the target line for that brief moment called *impact.*

Step Six

Once I'm confident that my body and the club are *square,* I bend over from the ball-and-socket joints of the hips while keeping my knees relatively straight, but not locked. As I bend to the ball, I let my buttocks extend out a bit to counterbalance the weight of the upper body, which is now a little farther forward since I'm bending over more. This allows me to set my weight into my hips, not my knees.

If you look at yourself in the mirror, you'll see a vast difference between this *new* posture and the classic address position. By keeping your legs straighter and bending more at the hips, you create a sharper angle between the legs and spine—it should be about 30 degrees. This posture ensures that you stand the right distance from the ball and also enables the body to turn more freely going back and coming down into the ball. It creates the proper angle of address at which 95 percent of all the work in the golf swing is done.

In setting up to drive, it's paramount that you bend from the ball-and-socket joints of the hips to create a 30-degree angle between your legs and spine. This posture enables the body to coil more freely going back and uncoil more freely coming down.

Step Seven

I confirm that, on a scale of one to ten, my grip pressure is five. The pressure in your hands should be firm enough to control the weight of the club, but not so tight that the natural swinging motion is inhibited. Don't apply added pressure to the last two fingers of the left hand and middle two fingers of the right hand, as is commonly taught. The weight of the club changes with the speed at different points in the swing; therefore the hands will naturally grip more firmly or loosely depending on what stage of the swing you are in.

Step Eight

Once I feel totally comfortable that I've cloned the ideal setup position I practice over and over, and over again, I then focus once more on the target area—my imaginary swimming pool—and visualize the ball splashing into it for a second time.

I'm not a believer in looking down at the ball, then up at the target, more than once at this stage. The reason: I might notice hazards that I've already mentally blocked out, therefore putting unnecessary doubt in my head and unneeded tension in my body.

Step Nine

I initiate my backswing by letting my right knee extend and my left knee flex. Simultaneously, my shoulders and chest begin turning behind the ball. This very natural body motion allows my center of gravity to begin the swing instead of the outside perimeter. Remember, the axle turns the wheel, the wheel doesn't turn the axle.

MIKE DUNAWAY'S MASTER CLASS

GET A GRIP

When good players slump, high scores can often be traced to a duck-hook problem. Instead of the ball flying straight off the clubface and directly at the target, it flies left, then darts left even more.

If you are experiencing the duck-hook blues, check your grip. You could be holding the club with your left hand turned too far to the right—away from the target. This fault makes you swing on an overly flat plane and, ultimately, close the clubface at impact.

To check your grip, stand at address and look down at your left hand. If you see three or more knuckles, you've gripped the club wrong. To *neutralize* your strong grip and correct your shotmaking fault, turn your left hand toward the target until you can see only two to two and one-half knuckles.

READY, SET, GO

Having played with many club golfers over the years and having carefully observed their setups and swings, I think the average player spends too much time at address, readying himself to hit.

Granted, it's important to jockey your body into a comfortably correct position, and to confirm that the club is square to a distant target, but that's where the setup should stop and the swing should begin. If you keep moving around, adjusting and readjusting your body and club positions, you run the risk of moving yourself out of position.

Try this little experiment to prove to yourself the value of a quick, correct setup: Go out on the course in the late afternoon when it's quiet and hit two balls on each driving hole. On the first shot, get set quickly and swing. On the second ball, take extra time, tinkering with your setup. Record the differences. I'll bet the first ball wins every time!

KEEP YOUR CHIN UP

Many amateur golfers know that a steady head position is fundamental to all great ball strikers. Yet, some misinterpret the familiar tip, "Keep your head down," and tilt their heads so far down that the chin touches the chest. This posturing surely steadies the head (it locks it in position), but it prevents you from rotating your left shoulder freely under your chin and making a strong upper body coil. The result: a weak shot.

To ensure a good turn of the shoulders, keep your head down, but *your chin up*.

FREE YOUR LEFT HIP

Turning the left hip freely on the backswing is critical to creating a strong upper body coil and opening a clear passageway for the arms, hands, and club to swing on the backswing. However, many golfers, particularly senior players who lack flexibility, have great difficulty employing a free hip turn.

If you have a problem turning your left hip on the backswing, move the toe-end of your left foot to the left—*away* from the target line in the setup. (If the toe was at 90 degrees to the target line in the setup, move it 10 to 20 degrees farther right to give yourself more freedom to turn.)

This small adjustment will make a big difference to the power you generate.

SMART START

Many high-handicap golfers get so caught up trying to think out technique that they have trouble actually starting the club away from the ball.

If you're a player who is baffled by numerous backswing thoughts, try this one simple thought: "Finish the backswing."

Repeat those three words slowly to yourself when setting up and you won't suffer from paralysis-by-analysis anymore. You'll swing right *through* the takeaway and be on your way to making a truly effortless power swing.

PLAY BALL

When analyzing your game after a round of eighteen holes, if you've determined that your inconsistent drives flew extra high and not very far, and faded off to the right, too, you're probably playing the ball too far back in your stance—closer to the midway point between your feet. Playing the ball back that far is fine if you're preparing to hit a wedge shot, and want to hit down sharply for more backspin. However, that ball position will not work when you want to hit a long drive.

On drives, you must sweep the ball on the *upswing*. Therefore, the ball must be played somewhere between your left heel and left instep. Correct your faulty ball position and you'll find reviewing your round at the nineteenth hole is a lot sweeter.

"PLANE" AND SIMPLE

No golfer should swing on an exaggerated flat plane, unless he's purposely playing a fancy shot around an obstacle. Having said that, a short player should swing on a more rounded, slightly flatter plane than a person of medium-tall height.

If you are under 5 feet 7 inches, and want to guarantee that you swing on "your" plane, then stand to the ball so that there is about a foot of air space between your body and the butt end of the club. Golfers who are 5 feet 7 inches to 5 feet 9 inches should set up with a one-hand gap between their body and the butt end of the club. Taller players who want to ensure a very upright plane should set up with even less space between their body and the top end of the club.

HOW OVERWEIGHT GOLFERS CAN BEAT THE "FLATS"

Golfers who are overweight have a tendency to swing back under their stomach on far too flat a plane. The only way to hit the ball straight from that faulty backswing position is to make some sort of compensatory movement on the downswing and time the shot perfectly. That truly is easier said than done.

If you have a big belly, you need to guard against swinging on an overly flat plane by assuming a slightly open alignment, aiming your feet, knees, hips, and shoulders a bit left of target. Don't overdo it.

This setup will make you swing short of parallel, and on an upright plane. Because you'll come into the ball from a position slightly outside the target line, you'll consistently hit a controlled power shot that moves a little from left to right.

STAY IN LINE

Beginners at golf often position their hands too far ahead of the ball when playing a driver. They tell me this gives them a sense of strength and power. I tell them that's probably true, but an exaggerated hands-ahead position at address will not produce powerful drives.

Setting up with your hands in front of the ball causes you to lean left at address. What's worse, this fault causes you to hit the ball with most of your weight on your right foot instead of your left. Therefore, you can't ever make a solid hit at impact.

When you set up to drive, be sure your hands are *in line* with the ball (or slightly behind it). You might feel powerless, but you'll hit powerful shots.

USE YOUR IMAGINATION

Narrow fairways usually frighten the typical high-handicap golfer and cause him to coax the swing in an attempt to hit the ball straight. Ironically, in trying to "steer" the ball down the fairway, he hits a wild shot.

Powerful golf shots are a direct result of an *uninhibited* strong swing motion. However, I realize how intimidating tight tree-lined fairways can be. Frankly, I don't like them all that much either. Here's a tip that should help.

As you address the ball, picture the fairway as a two-lane highway with cars traveling along it. The realization that if two automobiles can fit in the fairway, one little golf ball surely can, will relax you and enable you to make a free-flowing good swing.

PROPER EXTENSION

One of the worst errors a golfer can commit is to pick up the club quickly in the initial stage of the swing. This fault makes you swing the club on such a dramatically steep backswing plane that you fail to turn your upper body. In turn, you create a reverse weight shift that totally destroys power and direction.

The hands should set before your left arm reaches the first horizontal position. The right angle must be established between the left arm and shaft to create a proper extension without moving the head off the ball.

SET UP "RIGHT"

A good shift of weight onto the right side is essential to "loading" the body with stored power on the backswing.

On the downswing, when weight shifts back to the left side, this power is transmitted through the arms, hands, clubshaft, and finally the clubhead!

If you feel you're not hitting the ball quite as far as you should, or as long as you have in the past, give yourself a head start to storing power on the backswing by setting up with slightly more weight on your *right* foot.

TAKE DEAD AIM

Aligning the clubface squarely to the target is a technical *must* for producing powerful, accurate drives. Yet many amateur golfers sole the clubface down incorrectly, so that it looks left or right of the target. Consequently, the ball is hit into trouble bordering the fairway.

To help you achieve your goal of lining up correctly, place your ball down on the tee peg so that its label runs horizontally (as you look down) *along the target line.*

Now, your good swings will no longer hit the ball off line.

PRE-CLEAR YOUR LEFT HIP

Once your right hip pushes downward to trigger the downswing, your left hip must quickly respond and "clear" to the left (away from the target), in order to open a clear path for the arms and hands to bring the club into the ball.

Some golfers, particularly those players who did not participate in ball sports during their youth, have less agile bodies that are slow to respond. In fact, if you've been hitting drives that drift off target, your problem could very well be a slow-clearing left hip. If so, try these two tips. When you set up:

- Rotate the toe-end of your left foot out about 30 degrees from a position perpendicular to the target line.
- Turn your left hip slightly to the left. Now that your hips are in a *pre-cleared* position, you'll find it easy to swing through with the sweet spot of the club meeting the ball.

SQUARE UP YOUR STANCE

Golfers who slice tend to toy with their swings on the practice tee, trying to trace and correct a swing fault. Sometimes they spend hours at the range trying numerous swing tips that don't help. Why? The fault is in the *setup,* not the swing.

If you consistently hit slices off the tee, address a ball and aim to a target. Then have a friend lay a club across your feet. Stand back. If your feet aim well left of an imaginary line running from the ball to the target, your problem is setting up too *open.* A severe open stance will cause you to swing the club from out-to-in and cut across the ball at impact.

Practice until you groove a square stance (feet parallel to target line). Then, you'll make "straight-ball" swings, not "slice-ball" swings.

PARALLEL YOUR SHOULDERS

One setup fault common to country club golfers is pointing their shoulders at the target. Although, logically, this position might seem right, it is not.

Unless you're setting up to hit a hook shot, address the ball with your shoulders *parallel* to the target line—not pointing at it. This is the only way to promote the proper inside-square-inside clubhead path and a pure hit.

TOTAL RECALL

Many golfers who seek long distance off the tee make the mistake of focusing down on the ball too long at address. Becoming "ball bound" does two detrimental things:

- It breeds unnecessary tension in the body, particularly the arms, which are key to whipping the club into the ball.
- It makes you try to hit *at* the ball, instead of *through* it.

The best way to relax your body at address is to recall the great tee shots you have hit in the past.

2

THE POWER BACKSWING

Slowly winding the body into a compact position helps you store power and readies you for a hard hit

Now that you have learned the vital steps to setting up properly, you know how critical a correct address is to making a good swing and hitting the ball hard. What you do not know, however, is this: As important as the setup is, it is not the be-all and end-all of learning how to hit solid drives that fly on the designated line and trajectory your mind's eye visualizes before you swing. A lot of things must go right between the time you trigger the swing and hit the ball.

This chapter concerns the how-to's of the backswing, which is the segment of the swing that starts when you take the club away from the ball and ends when you arrive at the top, with the clubshaft paralleling the ball-target line. The essence of the backswing, or the "retreat" position, as I call it, is to wind up and ready yourself to spring back and whip the club into the ball. For the backswing to work as efficiently as possible, with the movement of the club in sync with the movement of the body, you must possess good tempo and timing.

Tempo is simply the speed of the swing. Timing is the sequence of the swing motion. Timing relies on good tempo. Ideally, you should swing with a tempo that allows you to control the club, while keeping the body in a state of balance. Furthermore, if you swing at a controlled speed, you will give yourself enough time for all of the pieces of the motion to fall into place.

Before teaching you the fine points of my backswing technique, let me tell you how to *feel* the proper sequence of the motion, which involves simultaneously working six pairs of skeletal joints: two ankles, two knees, two hips, two shoulders, two elbows, and two wrists. The way you'll learn to feel the motion is by performing a unique drill that operates according to the same basic principles that govern the mechanics of the golf swing.

This drill requires two props that can be purchased at any hardware store: an eight-foot piece of rope and a large-sized eye bolt.

THE A-FRAME DRILL

In setting up the simple apparatus, securely place the eye bolt in your backyard lawn; then thread the rope through it.

Next, hold an end of the rope in each hand. Let some excess rope wrap around your hands, so you have a secure hold. Pull the ends taut so they form an A-frame, the sides of which are about 44 inches—the length of my driver.

Now, jockey your body into the same basic setup position prescribed in the previous chapter. To review, you'll want to:

- Spread your feet shoulder-width apart.
- Balance your weight on the arches of each foot.
- Angle out the toe-end of your left foot more than your right foot.
- Align your feet, knees, hips, and shoulders parallel to an imaginary target line.
- Bend at the ball-and-socket joints of the hips to a 30 degree angle and keep your knees straight—not locked.
- Let your arms extend in a relaxed fashion.

The A-frame drill will give you a good feel for the basic mechanics of the backswing.

- Set your hands about eight inches away from your body.

Once you feel comfortable and correct, simultaneously extend the right knee and turn your right shoulder away from the pulley. Stop when your right shoulder has turned well behind your left, your back faces an imaginary target, and your shoulders have rotated 90 degrees. Return to the address position and repeat the drill ten times.

While doing this drill, feel how your body coils like a big spring and how freely your joints work together in a coordinated fashion. One movement leads to another movement—not unlike a row of dominoes falling over one by one, once the "fall" is triggered by a gentle movement of the first domino.

As you perform this drill, the left hip drops slightly as the lower spine moves a shade to the right, causing the upper spine to tilt slightly left. That small tilt is the essence of this drill and, more important, the *backswing,* because it sets the spine at the proper angle for the shoulders to turn correctly. (In the backswing, my left shoulder and arm rotate on a slightly downward incline. My right shoulder also rotates on an incline, back and up. As I complete the backswing, I want to feel that I've turned my back to the target, or that my back is *behind the ball.*) Winding your shoulder blades identically with the way you do in the A-frame rope drill adds 20 to 30 degrees to the turn, thereby enabling you to generate the power you've been searching for. If you assume the correct posture when addressing the ball and stay tension-free as you rotate your left hip at the start of the swing (and drill), this turning power should happen naturally, which is the beauty of this technique.

Practicing this drill on a daily basis will definitely help you get a feel for the basic movements involved in swinging the golf club back to the at-the-top position. However, an intellectual grasp of the complex movements is crucial to power golf, too, just as learning the location of the keys on a typewriter is the first step to typing 60 words a minute without having to think about what the fingers are doing. For this reason, what follows is a detailed account of my backswing technique—the first step to playing *automatic power golf.*

BACKSWING TECHNIQUE

At the initial stage of the backswing, called the "takeaway," I coil my left hip and upper back in a clockwise direction, and pilot the club around the plane of the address position. This swing trigger enables me to direct the club straight back along the correct path and up on the correct plane, which are two critical elements to hitting accurate tee shots. Furthermore, my left hip coil promotes the correct pivot action, which is critical to hitting the ball powerfully.

Balance changes during the golf swing. At address, you stand on a two-foot balance; at the top, you're on a one-foot balance on your extended right leg; at impact, you're once again on a one-foot balance, this time on your extended left leg; and at the finish position, you remain on a one-foot balance.

You probably don't realize it, but you practice the correct body movements for a golf swing several hundred times a day. Whenever you take a step forward with your left foot, your right shouler naturally moves back. When you take a step forward with your right foot, your left shoulder naturally moves back. If you walk in balance, your head will stay relatively steady.

If you begin your golf swing by turning the right hip, you will automatically create a reverse weight shift and make the clubhead move off the ball to the right. To get back to square will require manufacturing added moves to your swing.

The correct pivot action is difficult for the untrained eye to absorb. The best way to learn the correct pivot action is to place your buttocks against a wall in your address position. Immediately you will notice that you cannot turn your right hip, because of the wall. What you can do is let your left hip swing away from the wall and rotate it around the right leg. This will create a winding-up motion of the right hip. As the left hip moves off the wall, your right shoulder will move naturally behind your neck. This Pivot-Hip drill ensures a steady head and proper balance.

As the downswing begins, the Wall drill is repeated and reversed. At the top of the swing, the first motion is not the

The overall rhythm of your swing is established here, in the takeaway, so the club must be started back smoothly along the target line. Quietly rotating your left hip clockwise will promote an even tempo.

turning back of the left hip. You must shift your weight laterally left and let the right hip and knee rotate around the left leg. The left hip cannot and does not work *into* the wall, but *to* the wall. This pivot action creates a winding, torquing motion that puts the body in its most powerful position to deliver a blow.

The smoother the turning action of the left hip around the right leg, the more unified is the takeaway action, involving the hands, wrists, arms, and shoulders.

If you combine the A-Frame drill and the Wall drill, you are on your way to learning how to strike the golf ball solidly. The golf swing is most effective when all twelve major joints are working together without an exaggerated effort to offset a weak pattern. This pivot action makes the body swing the hands and clubhead, not the reverse.

The best way to comprehend the plane the club swings on is to imagine, as Ben Hogan did, that your head is poking through a hole in a big plane of glass resting on your shoulders and touching the ground, just past the ball at its bottom end. Ideally, you should swing the club back on this exact plane. But don't forget that at address your arms and shaft are below the plane; you get on the proper plane only when the left arm reaches its first horizontal position on the backswing. This correct plane allows you to swing the club easily and more consistently along the target line for that brief flashing moment, called impact.

Many high-handicap golfers confuse an upright backswing plane with a straight-up type of swing. Don't make that mistake, because then you will lift the arms too abruptly, and look like Paul Bunyan chopping wood at impact. For the correct arc to pay off in terms of effortless power, it must be accompanied by an extended left arm created by a full turn of the shoulder and proper support of the right leg. One extremely important measurement in the golf swing is the distance from the ball to the spine. Most people believe that the spine is located in the middle of the body, so mentally they try to swing around it. This is incorrect. The spine is located on the *back* of the body. The measurement of the left arm to the ball must also include the width of the chest. This gives your chest room to turn around your spine and not into it.

Until my takeaway is completed, with the clubshaft and left arm horizontal and parallel to the target line, I'm very careful not to move laterally, or "off the ball." The reason is I know only too well how easily this fault can cause an overly steep backswing arc and a reciprocal sharp downward hit at impact, rather than a powerful upswing sweep. The result: a slice shot that flies right of your target area. I'm also careful not to turn my gentle clockwise hip turn into a violent spin. Spinning the hips causes you to swing on an overly "flat" plane. Then, that rounded type of swing

Allowing your right elbow to hinge naturally late in the takeaway promotes a more controlled upright swing plane.

usually causes you to roll the clubface into such a closed position at impact that you inevitably hit a hook shot left of target. To guard against both of those faults, I keep my head perfectly still and my lower body relatively quiet early in the backswing.

While my shoulders and upper body start to coil more fully, the section of my torso just below my waist feels what I can best describe as *comfortably tense.* The reason is that I never allow my head to pass my belly button as I coil my upper body against my lower body. Coiling the upper body against a resisting lower body allows you to create torque and extend the left-arm–clubshaft unit into the horizontal position that signifies the end of the takeaway. Of course, I can't see the club swing back to the first parallel position (at waist level). But I can sure feel my weight shift into my right hip and also feel my right wrist "give" from the swinging force of the clubhead. These are my signals to start swinging upward.

At this stage in my swing, I feel that the club is being piloted on the desired upright plane by my swinging arms and on an inside path by my shoulders that turn at right angles to my spine. As my shoulders continue rotating in a clockwise fashion, my right arm flexes at the elbow and my right wrist cocks, which helps me keep the club traveling "on plane." It's then that I rotate my right hip a bit more briskly, making room for my arms and club to swing up freely.

As I continue turning my upper body, more weight shifts to my right side, causing my right leg to straighten. The right knee has to come into an extension to support the upper body properly. Besides, extending the knee creates a brace for me to coil against as the club moves toward the "top." The firmer the brace, the tighter the turn. The tighter the turn, the more stored power is created within the springlike coil of the upper body. (If you employ the correct backswing action, you will feel your left foot wanting to lift off the ground. Unless you lack flexibility, leave

As you swing farther back you'll feel your right leg want to straighten. Let it; it serves as a brace for you to coil against.

it planted on the grass, as this will further strengthen your turn and provide you with even more stored power to unleash on the downswing in the form of clubhead speed.)

The clubshaft's position at the top of the backswing generally indicates the direction the drive will fly. Ideally, the clubshaft should be parallel to the target line; that is the best position from which to deliver the clubhead straight along the target line and squarely into the ball. (If, at the top, the club points left of target—in a *laid-off* position—you'll probably swing into the ball from outside the target line and hit a shot that flies left of where you aimed. If the shaft points right of target—in a *cross-the-line* position—the forward swing arc will likely return the clubhead to the ball from inside to outside the target line, thereby creating a push shot that flies right.)

Another one of my top-of-the-backswing goals is to have my hand-wrist unit set in a secure position no higher than my head and no lower than my right shoulder. If my hands are too high, my swing plane is too upright; too low and my swing plane is too flat. (To correct an overly steep backswing plane, work on rotating your shoulders in a more clockwise direction. To correct an overly flat plane, practice swinging your hands more skyward than behind you on the backswing.)

Being in the ideal position at the top also means the shoulders are turned 90 degrees and the hips 30 degrees from their starting angles at address. At this point, my back should fully face the target and I should feel winding pressure in my right hip. In reading this, surely some of you golfers who have been taught that a 45-degree hip turn is important to power golf are confused by how little I turn my hips. So, let me explain:

If I make a big windup with my hips on the backswing, no lively tension is created in the midsection muscles of the stomach, back, and shoulders. Now, that might sound like a good thing, but it's a bad thing. A golfer needs some amount of tension in this area of his body; this is what will allow his upper body to spring back more naturally and powerfully on the downswing. That springing action promotes a slinging action of the arms on the downswing which, in turn, allows you to direct the club into the ball at *controlled* high speed.

Ideally, at the top of the swing, the clubshaft should be perfectly parallel to the target line.

MIKE DUNAWAY'S MASTER CLASS

TO LIFT OR NOT TO LIFT THE LEFT HEEL

I advocate lifting the left heel on the backswing only to golfers who lack flexibility and can't otherwise reach the classic parallel position at the top of the swing.

Be careful, however; there is a vast difference between allowing the left heel to lift and lifting it consciously.

If you feel the pull of the turn is *forcing* your left heel off the ground, don't resist. However, don't ever deliberately lift your left heel off the ground; then you run the risk of raising up—coming out of your coil and losing power in the process.

WRIST ACTION

Beginners always ask me, "When is the right time to cock the wrists on the backswing?" The wrist begins to cock after the left arm passes the right leg and must be completed by the time the leg and arm are in a horizontal position to the ground. But beware of thinking consciously about the wrist cock; that could lead to trying to swing too much with your hands and wrists.

To create a wide and powerful swing arc, you must have an extended left arm and a full shoulder turn.

THE "INSIDE" SCOOP

The majority of amateur golfers realize that, in order to sweep the club powerfully into the ball, it must first be guided back low to the ground and on an inside path. However, they don't realize that it's a technical *no-no* to pull the club violently inside the target line.

Whether you are a beginner or a high handicapper who

has been playing for a while, understand right now that the only right way to swing the club inside the target line on the backswing and hit with a powerful sweeping action is to turn the shoulders in a clockwise direction and let the hands follow the arc created by that shoulder turn.

To convince yourself that your *turning shoulders*—not your hands—swing the club to the "inside" automatically, set the head of a driver against the base of a wall and grip the club. Turn your shoulders and watch the club move away from the wall and swing to the inside.

THE OTHER HALF

If you're one of those golfers who has tested every tip for turning your body on the backswing, and none have worked, try this: Pretend that a line stretching from the base of your neck down your spine divides your left and right sides. The left half is elastic; the right half is cement. Stretch those *elastic bands* by turning your left side, making a powerful windup.

BE A NATURAL

If you're tall, don't make the mistake of trying to swing on an upright plane by pulling the club straight up toward the sky in the takeaway. Do that and you'll inevitably steepen the plane, chop down at impact, and hit the ball into rough or woods.

Instead, after properly setting up relatively close to the ball, let the lie of the club and the *natural* swinging action of your arms take it to the top.

BE A "SMOOTHY"

In trying to hit a ball extra hard, the average golfer reaches a point of diminishing returns. The typical player swings the club so very fast in the takeaway that by the time he reaches impact, the club is decelerating. This quick-takeaway/slow-clubhead-speed relationship is analogous to a marathon runner sprinting full-out for the first mile of the race and finishing behind the pack.

You'll never hit firmly through the ball at impact unless you start the club back *smoothly* and graduate to maximum *acceleration.* Remember, good tempo means swinging at the maximum speed at which you can *control* the club.

STOP THE SWAY

Allowing your upper body to rock laterally away from the target—to *sway*—definitely destroys your turning power and throws off your timing, too. The result: misdirected shots that fly a short distance. Three solutions to your sway problem follow:

- Imagine there is a six-foot wooden stake stuck in the ground, about six inches to the right of your right leg. Without a club in your hands, turn your right hip clockwise so that you avoid the imaginary stake.
- Point the toe-end of your right foot inward to discourage excess leg action.
- In practice, hit drives with a golf ball under your right foot to help the right side serve as a *solid* brace.

STAY COMPACT

Overswinging is a major fault shared by club-level golfers. Every player wants to hit the ball far, but since an overly long swing throws the body's natural chain reaction out of sync, I recommend you keep your action compact. Never swing the club beyond the classic parallel position at the top.

One sure way to control the length of your backswing is to pretend that you are trying to hit the ball only 100 yards with a driver.

PICTURE PERFECT

The position of the left wrist at the top of the swing seems insignificant to many novice golfers. Most of them, however, finish the backswing with their left wrist in a convex position. That fault forces the clubface to point skyward, which means it is closed to the swing plane. It also means that you will not be able to release the club at high speed; thus the faulty wrist position creates a serious power leak.

To ensure that you are in the best position to deliver the club powerfully into the ball, assume a good grip and practice until you can reach the top with your left wrist firm and flat—in line with your left forearm. That's the picture-perfect position common to almost all solid hitters.

GET HIP

There has been so much golf instruction written about turning the shoulders on the backswing that some amateur players forget to turn their hips. I accept that the shoulders should turn more than the hips, but if you freeze the hips, you'll cheat yourself out of vital power.

Turning the hips correctly is what allows you to coil the body more *tightly,* like a spring, on the backswing and unwind more powerfully on the downswing.

3

THE POWER DOWNSWING

Pushing the right hip forward between the left leg and the ball triggers a dynamic power release of the body and the club

The main purpose of the backswing is to slowly coil the body into a technically sound, compact, and comfortable position. The main purpose of the downswing is to powerfully unravel the body and whip the club squarely into the back center portion of the ball at maximum high speed, while maintaining postural poise and optimal balance.

In trying to present easy-to-follow instruction, I have chosen to describe the backswing and downswing separately, tearing my swing down to the bare bones, explaining each and every critical movement in clear detail. However, I truly believe that these two simple-looking, seemingly isolated actions—one going up and away from the ball, one going down and through the ball—must be rhythmically married into one uninterrupted flowing motion. For this reason, particularly, I think many modern-day golf teachers mislead students by advising them to pause at the top of the swing.

Pausing at the top of the backswing prompts a player to consciously depend upon some type of unorthodox trigger—i.e., an overly forceful lunge with the body—to launch the downswing. Consequently the possibility of making a smooth transition into the downswing is destroyed, and with that, the swing's natural chain reaction is thrown out of sync.

The two most classic examples of the inappropriate use of downswing triggers by club-level amateur golfers who pause at the top involve improper movements of the shoulders and hands.

The golfer who consistently hits tee shots very high and a very short distance, with a slice pattern, wrongly initiates the downswing by violently thrusting his right shoulder downward and over the toe-line. The reason he commits this fault is that he pauses too long at the top and thus finds it extremely difficult to make a natural lower-body shift to the left side. Consequently, in a desperate attempt to swing down and through the ball, he dips his shoulder, comes well under the ball with the clubface open (aiming right) and hits a weak slice shot.

Another common bad shot club golfers hit—a "duck hook" that flies left off the clubface and quickly darts farther left during flight—can also be caused by pausing at the top of the swing. Once the golfer reaches the top and stops, his lower body freezes. Because there is no tug of the lower body toward the target (as there is when the backswing and downswing blend into one continual motion), the right hip does not push downward as it should, and the arms do not move outward from the body and whip the club through the hit zone, as they should. Under these circumstances, the player, who obviously feels helpless, has little choice but to futilely flail the club at the ball with his hands. This aggressive hand action causes the clubface to close or look left of target, with the result being a hook shot.

I cite these two examples of bad shots, not to criticize the club golfer but to emphasize one fact: *The golf swing is designed to be one fluid motion, and when you disrupt its flow by pausing at the top, you mistime the return of the club into the ball and mishit the shot.*

Conversely, when a golfer's timing is good and he makes a smooth transition from the top into the downswing, he is in full control of the club in the hitting area, where it definitely counts most. The clubhead swings into the ball at high speed, aiming straight at the target. The contact is solid and the flight according to plan.

I admit to sensing a slight pause at the top of the backswing. But I know from scrutinizing sequence photographs of my swing, shot with a high-speed camera, that the split second the club arrives in the classic parallel position (at the top), my lower body springs back involuntarily toward the target, triggering the downward motion. Therefore, when I feel a pause I'm really feeling a *lag,* as my shoulders, arms, hands, and club reverse direction and play catch-up with the lower body, once it starts leading me into the downswing.

It only takes me approximately a fifth of a second to deliver the club from the top of the swing to the ball. Therefore, once my downswing is sparked by a downward pushing action with my right hip, and my body starts unraveling, there's no going back. Because this interplay of the neuromuscular system is so complex, and the downswing so fast, this hip trigger of mine is more an involuntary action than a conscious movement.

To acquaint yourself with the feel of the shoulders, arms, and hands playing catch-up with the lower body, repeat the same *rope exercise* described in the previous chapter, only this time begin from the backswing position, when you are fully wound up. Once you feel that your body is ready to spring back toward the target—due to the extent of the upper body coil and the tension in your midsection—push your right hip downward, and counter-

The A-frame drill will quickly familiarize you with the "feels" involved in the downswing.

clockwise toward the golf ball and left leg. Instantly, you will feel the key movements involved in the downswing. The right hip unwinds and drops slightly, while the right arm and hand move quickly outward, readying themselves to release the club into the ball.

The transition from the backswing into the downswing is the most important stage of the golf swing—where all the action takes place. However, the entire downswing (from the moment the club changes direction to the moment the ball is hit) is reflexive, meaning that its integral movements are merely a reflection of those that came previously. Since the entire downward motion happens so quickly—literally in the blink of an eye—if you are out of position there is absolutely nothing you can do consciously to correct the misdirected path the club is traveling along. Which is precisely why I have already stressed to you the vital importance of setting up correctly and swinging back into a sound at-the-top position.

Once my downswing has been triggered, my body and the club go into an automatic-pilot mode. Furthermore, because practically the entire downswing is controlled by the subconscious mind, it would be truly farcical for me to deem any one of its movements, simultaneously involving the movements of all twelve joints, a swing principle or *key* that you could practice and groove. After all, I can't stop at any one point during the speedy chain action, correct a faulty position, and resume the swing. All the same, knowing what each correct downswing position looks like, and where it fits into the sequence helps me—as it will you—correctly piece together a free-flowing motion.

Even though, after pushing your right hip downward and springing back toward the target, you can't consciously put yourself in any one of the correct downswing positions, I truly believe that by describing each one, I will help you visualize the proper sequential motion, and with time

Pushing the right hip down and toward the target triggers the downswing.

and hard practice, you will be able to physically clone my action. Here is what a sophisticated sequence camera tells me happens in my downswing, the moment my body starts to unravel:

1. My right hip pushes downward between the left leg and the ball, causing the left hip to move laterally, setting up the support of the torso. This enables the right hip and leg to rotate counterclockwise around toward the target.
2. My left hip moves laterally toward the target.
3. My hands direct the shaft and clubhead between the wrist and ball, maintaining the proper swing plane. (Here is when I first feel stored energy readying itself to be released into the clubhead, via my arms, hands, and then the clubshaft.)
4. As my left hip starts the forward movement, my right hip and knee simultaneously move counterclockwise around the left leg.
5. My right shoulder angle remains constant in relation to the right side of the rib cage. The right hip chases the right elbow—not the reverse. In still photography, because the right side is rotating toward the ball, it looks as if the elbow is being tucked into the right hip. This is only an illusion.
6. As weight shifts dramatically to my left foot, I feel the rotation of the torso advancing my left arm on the correct plane to the golf ball. I do *not* pull down with the left arm.
7. I feel my left shoulder returning from a low position at the top of the backswing to a higher position at impact.
8. As my left shoulder moves up, my right shoulder moves down. Both shoulders rotate around the 30 degree angle created by the spine at address.

9. My left thigh rotates counterclockwise around an extended left leg. My left hip doesn't open to the target, my right hip closes into and toward the target. This creates tremendous forward rotation and power.
10. My left elbow rotates underneath the left arm to allow the knuckles of the left hand to hit the back center of the golf ball at impact.
11. It is very important that you do not lock the left wrist at impact; just the opposite occurs. Total relaxation of the inside muscles of the left forearm and wrist allows the shaft and clubhead to pick up additional acceleration through the hitting area. The left arm and shaft create one common line that is directly on the plane line of impact. This position maximizes the delivery of the centrifugal force built up by the swing.
12. As the club swings from well inside the target line, back to the ball, my hands-arm unit makes a sidearm motion. (At this point, I feel as if I'm swinging outward and energy is traveling speedily through my arms.) I am also aiming my clubhead at the inside quadrant of the golf ball.
13. While my left shoulder moves farther up and the rotation of the right hip around the left leg occurs, my head remains on center-line between my two feet, allowing the clubhead to swing through the golf ball up the target line on the plane. The secret to balance is simply to keep your head between your feet.
14. As my right arm and right wrist straighten out at impact, my right hand speed increases and likewise the centrifugal force.
15. BOOM! The sweetspot of the clubface smashes the ball, just as it's starting to swing upward at the very bottom of its arc.

Keeping your head down in the hitting area is the only true way to preserve the downswing's chain reaction.

Now, can you imagine trying to think of all those things to do during the swing? Of course not! Reading those steps should reassure any golfer of one truism of technique: *The downswing is far too fast and complex an action to be consciously directed.*

Having, I hope, proved my point, I frankly think it is a sheer waste of time for a golfer to segregate any one of the complex body-club positions involved in the downswing and practice it separately as if it were an isolated "secret move." What is very worthwhile, however, is to work diligently at drumming my right-sided trigger (pushing the right hip downward and counterclockwise around the left leg) into your muscle memory. When you reach the top and feel compelled to spring back down, that one trigger will serve as a catalyst and allow you to automatically swing into and *through* all of the paramount positions or *links* of the downswing's connected chain.

The downswing should not be a consciously directed action, but rather a subconscious activity that allows me to make a smooth transition into the downswing and deliver the club squarely into the ball. My secret: I *trust* correct clubface-to-ball contact at impact to be a direct result of all the correct previous moves I made before starting the downswing. This confidence is what allows me to *let go*—to let the swing happen once my right hip *involuntarily* pushes downward and rotates around the left leg. I must go out of control to gain control.

Throughout my golfing life, I've hit thousands upon thousands of balls on the practice tee. And this is precisely why I'm confident that my downswing switches to cruise control the split second it is triggered. In fact, I'm so confident I believe that if I let the swing happen naturally the ball will get in the way of a good swing. Maybe that explains why I actually blank out until after impact, when I look up and see the ball zooming off the clubface, then flying upward fast toward the target, some 300 yards down the fairway.

The follow-through technically begins a split second after impact.

Good arm-club extension through impact confirms that you released your right side correctly and powerfully.

I caution you not to think, when reading about my blanking out, that I advocate taking the eyes off the ball. Even though "the hit" is an instantaneous, quick flash, which you never see no matter how hard you focus your eyes on the ball, you still must keep your head down. Staying down is the only true way to preserve the natural chain action of the swing and, in doing so, hit a hard, dead-straight drive.

Regardless of how reflexive an action the downswing is, it's still essential to hit well through the ball at impact with optimum clubface-to-ball *penetration*. At the precise moment of impact, the ball is literally squished; then it spins off the clubface, ideally toward the target. The faster the club travels into the ball and the "squarer" the contact, the faster and farther the ball flies. The best avenue to achieving a solid squish of the ball and super-spin is to employ good extension in the follow-through.

The follow-through technically begins a split second after impact, when the right forearm, hand, and wrist gradually turn over. Nonetheless, because the follow-through is determined by the nature of the downswing, a golfer should have a good understanding of the movements leading up to this segment of the swing. Additionally, regardless of how reflexive the follow-through is, one should form a lucid image of the club being *slung* into the ball by the hands and arms. That kind of mental reinforcement, together with physically feeling the motion, is essential to accelerating the hands and arms and achieving good clubface-to-ball penetration. Let me, therefore, freeze the lead-in positions of the downswing that allow the follow-through to be technically pure, starting from the moment the hands are directed onto the swing plane.

A sidearm motion, very similar to that used by a second baseman throwing a baseball to first base, is what I use to thrust the club powerfully into the ball with good extension in the follow-through. Basically, as soon as my right

Finishing in a comfortably erect position, with the chest facing the target and the right foot vertical, is a true indication of a good, in-balance power swing.

hip pushes downward and starts to rotate around my left leg, I make a sidearm *slinging action.*

The parts of my body that play a big role during the sling and determine the degree of power and accuracy I ultimately produce on my drive are the upper right arm, lower right forearm, and the right hand. The body controls the upper action of the right arm, the extending of the elbow joint adds a second dimension of power to the swing, and the third action or lever is the releasing of the right hand freely to swing through the impact zone. The third can only occur if the left wrist is free also to hinge.

This in-tandem three-lever release, which is made much more powerful by a simultaneous hip and leg drive, is precisely what whips the club into impact, with its *sweet spot* squashing the back of the ball hard. The force of this downswing action is what allows you to achieve good extension of the club along the target line and have the clubface square to the back center of the ball at impact.

How you finish, more than how the ball flies, is the ultimate acid test of how well or how poorly you performed technically. That's because a golfer who employs a horrible-looking swing can occasionally hit a good shot. For this reason, check your finish.

If you end up standing comfortably erect and in balance, with your chest facing the target and the club slung over your left shoulder, you don't have to watch the ball's flight. Just walk on a straight line, far down the fairway.

MIKE DUNAWAY'S MASTER CLASS

BACK TO THE WALL

On the downswing the left leg must provide support, serving as an axis for the right side to pivot around. Controlling the pivot speed controls the power of the hit.

To maintain the axis that extends from your left shoulder blade to your left foot, keep your head behind the golf ball until the force of the club pulls you out of the angle of address.

SWING WITHIN YOURSELF

Because I give long-drive clinics at country clubs all over the world, I get to see many amateurs practice and play. I always get a kick out of eavesdropping on the conversations between golfers on the driving range. The tip I hear given the most is: "Swing down slowly."

The intention of giving such a tip is good but, frankly, it is misleading. Because the club swings into impact from inside the target line, it's difficult to return the clubface to a square impact position if you swing down in slow motion. If the lower body doesn't move quickly enough toward the target on the downswing, the upper body takes control and a mishit shot results. A much better tip for a fast swinger is: "Swing with maximum balance." That way, he will concentrate on maintaining good rhythm, and is dissuaded from swinging so fast that he loses control of the club.

PRESENT ARMS

Bad driving days on the golf course can sometimes be caused by consciously trying to pull the club into the ball. Often a player arrives at the "top" in the ideal position, then pulls violently down with the club as if he were tolling a church bell. This downswing action causes the club to come into the ball from such a steep angle that the ball usually flies well right of target.

To ensure that you come into the ball on a shallower angle of descent, forget about the hands and *accelerate the arms.*

ONE STEP BEYOND

Delivering the club squarely into the ball at maximum controlled speed is surely the key to hitting the ball hard and on target.

To ensure that you reach maximum acceleration at impact, convince yourself that the fastest point of the downswing is just *beyond* the ball. Then, there will be no chance of your decelerating the club at impact, where speed counts most.

BE RIGHT

Golf teachers, I think, overemphasize the importance of the left side in the downswing. Many claim golf is a game of opposites and that right-handed players need to direct the downswing with the left side. This, to me, is unnatural and probably a reason why so many golfers never reach their full potential as drivers of the ball.

Leaving the right side out of the downswing prevents you from accelerating the club to its maximum speed and hitting with all your weight behind the ball. So, make sure you *rotate* your right hip counterclockwise, around your left leg. Golf is a two-sided game.

COMPRESS THE BALL

Many golfers fail to achieve solid clubface-to-ball penetration at impact—they don't *compress* the ball for maximum distance—because they fail to release their right heel in the start of the downswing, preventing the proper hip motion.

A good way to ensure that you literally get a "boost" into impact (off your right foot) is to feel the muscles of your right rump pushing the right hip down and around the left leg with the right heel *over* the toes of the right foot.

RIGHT ELBOW CONTROL

The most common downswing fault is called "coming over the top." It means that at the start of the downswing, the player's right shoulder juts outward, causing him to hit across the ball, rather than down the target line.

If you constantly fight this fault, you are almost certainly backshifting the left hip, which throws the shoulder over the top instead of underneath and around. The left hip should advance laterally parallel to the target line. This will ensure the right shoulder won't cross over the toe-line established by the feet at address. The right shoulder should never cross this line before impact.

LET THE LOWER BODY LEAD THE HANDS AND ARM

One of the primary keys to effortless power golf is to swing the force, not force the swing. That's another way of saying you should just let things happen in the downswing. We want supple quickness, not rigid slowness.

Some club golfers wreck an otherwise good swing by stopping or slowing the pivotal action of the foreswing. If this occurs, you lose the elevation of your arms and an over-the-top action occurs. I don't think anybody has ever released a club too early; they simply make an incorrect pivot.

SWING SAVER

No matter how hard they practice, some golfers just can't seem to work themselves out of a steep backswing position—a virtual straight-up motion that leads to a sharp hit on the descent and a slice.

To correct this flaw, check your angle of address and make sure your arms and hands conform to the angle of the club. Most likely, you're much too upright at address and the sole of the golf club is not grounded properly. Check yourself in a mirror or on video.

SHOW AND TELL

The alignment of your body in the finish position of your swing will tell you a lot about your downswing technique.

Ideally, if you maintained good balance while swinging down, and good control of the club while accelerating it in the hitting zone, your right foot will be roughly in a vertical position at the finish, and your chest will be facing the target.

On the other hand, if your chest faces right of the target and most of your right foot is on the ground, you probably left the majority of your weight on your right foot.

To correct this fault—and your slice—shift your weight to the left side by rotating your right hip toward the target on the downswing, not backing up the left hip around the right.

4

DRILLWORK

A sure way to groove a sound power-driving technique

Having read to this point, you have observed the mechanics I employ to hit a golf ball far down the fairway. Given reasonable time and effort on the practice tee, you will physically groove all of the moves I taught you, and translate them into one free-flowing power swing. From that day on, you will experience a surprising and gratifying gain in distance off the tee.

It's important to keep in mind that an intellectual understanding of your new mechanics isn't all you need to create power. You need to completely retrain your muscles to unlearn the faulty, unorthodox movements you've ingrained over the years playing golf. You'll accomplish part of this retraining by hitting balls diligently and regularly on the practice tee, while adhering strictly to the key moves I've explained in the previous three chapters.

You can also train your various muscle groups to learn what they should be doing during the different parts of the golf swing through a series of specific drills I've developed. When you begin working on these drills you will probably feel downright clumsy for a while, but be patient and persevere, since that is the only true avenue to developing a powerfully graceful, uninhibited swing.

A good analogy to practicing these exercises is learning how to type. If you ever took a typing class in high school or college, surely you can remember how at first it seemed as though you'd never learn the typewriter's keyboard and how to cover all those keys—instinctively—with just ten fingers. Do you remember all those typing drills you didn't think you could handle if your life depended on it? If you're anything like me, you might have said to yourself more than once, "The heck with this, I'm going back to the old one-fingered, hunt-and-peck method. I'll be a lousy typist, but at least I'll know what I'm doing."

However, assuming you stuck with it, a day came when, almost like magic, everything seemed to click and your fingers started to move to the right keys as if they had a mind of their own. You probably couldn't believe it. Not only were you typing at a rate many times faster than you did with the hunt-and-peck method, but you were making far fewer mistakes.

Well, just as you'll type more efficiently when you don't have to think about hitting the keys one by one, so will you hit the golf ball longer and straighter when all the moves you need to execute have become instinctive. These drills will help you make the proper swing motions automatically. So, start working on them with enthusiasm and confidence.

DRILLS EMPHASIZE SQUARE CLUBHEAD DELIVERY

Before we begin, I'd like to make something clear. Contrary to what you might think I'd recommend to help you hit powerful golf shots, I am *not* going to send you to the gym and order you to perform a series of squats and bench presses. No, these drills are directed at developing the *quality* of your golf swing rather than raw physical power.

Keep in mind that a top-notch golf swing is one that

delivers the clubhead squarely into the ball at maximum speed.

It won't do you much good to generate a big increase in clubhead speed if your clubface-to-ball contact remains erratic. Greater clubhead speed will help you hit the ball farther only if the middle of the clubface, or "sweet spot," meets the back of the ball at impact. If the clubface is closed or open to the target line, you'll find yourself getting a lot wilder. And no golfer likes having to retee, and take a stroke-and-distance penalty, because his first drive flew far but over the out-of-bounds fence.

I can't emphasize enough how crucial it is to meet the ball as squarely as possible. This is the main source of increased distance. I guarantee you that every long driver contacts the ball very squarely as well as with exceptional clubhead speed. For this reason, I would classify only the first two of the following ten drills as strength-building exercises. The other eight will aid you in making the right technical moves that will lead to that all-important *square hit.*

DRILL 1: SWING A WEIGHTED DRIVER

Practicing your swinging action with a weighted driver is one of the best ways I know to strengthen all the key muscles that power the golf swing—back, hips, forearms, wrists, and hands. It's also a great way to train those muscles to move precisely as they must in order to deliver the clubface squarely to the back of the ball. Therefore, I believe training with a weighted driver is a drill you should do on the practice tee consistently, both before you play and after you play.

Many golfers think swinging two or three clubs at a time for a minute prior to starting a round is as valuable as hitting some practice balls on the range with a weighted driver. Let me say right now that swinging a couple of

Swinging a weighted club will help you strengthen those muscles vital to a power-golf technique.

clubs is *not* a sufficient alternative to hitting warm-up shots with a weighted driver. You need to feel that clubface-to-ball contact and get some basic feedback on the flight of the ball in order to organize your game plan for the day's round. Also, I do not advocate using two clubs as your "weighted" club for two other reasons. First, when you swing two or three clubs, you're hanging onto two or three grips instead of just one, which is cumbersome and foreign to formulating the proper hold on the club. Second, a weighted club has all of the additional weight located at or near the head of the club, which provides the greatest resistance to your swinging motions. Therefore, after warming up with a weighted driver your normal driver will feel so light you'll whip it into the ball at maximum speed. By comparison, two clubs will not feel much heavier than one in terms of "swingweight," even though their combined dead weight may be twice as much.

There are numerous handy devices for adding weight to a club that are available in nearly all pro shops and retail golf outlets. One is the plastic-coated metallic ring or "doughnut" that slips down the clubshaft and rests around the neck of the club. Or there are driver headcovers which have a small circular piece of lead sewn inside for added weight. Either of these items can instantly turn your driver into the perfect training tool.

You can also easily add permanent weight to an older driver in one of the following ways:

- Remove the sole plate of an old wood driver and apply solder to the sole of the club.
- Remove the club's grip and pour sand down the club-shaft. With either method, you can gradually increase the weight as your golf swing gets stronger.

Keep in mind that you do *not* need much extra weight on the clubhead, particularly at first. The "doughnut" or the weighted headcover each weighs only five to eight ounces. That should be sufficient extra weight for most handicap players to add to the club.

Whenever you're swinging a weighted club, remember to swing it *extra slowly*! The object is to feel the elements of the power swing and to stay in control of the clubhead and clubface despite the additional weight. Slow swings with the weighted club will also teach you good balance, which is critical to making solid contact with the ball at impact.

I recommend that all golfers swing a weighted club at home once or twice a week during the season. (For those who live in a northern region and face a long winter layoff, a weighted club workout every other day will work wonders come spring.) Start with about twenty slow, controlled repetitions. As your golf muscles get accustomed to the heavier load, you may wish to add a couple of extra ounces of weight and/or increase the number of repetitions. That's fine. Just remember to swing slowly and stay in control of that club from takeaway to follow-through.

DRILL 2: SWING A CLUB IN A POOL

The second exercise I advocate for developing swing strength as well as "memory" of the correct swing path is to swing a golf club in a pool of water. Granted, if you make use of a pool in your backyard, you may have to endure a few jokes from your neighbors to the effect that "the golf course is over that way." However, because "swinging in water" will ultimately help you hit the golf ball farther, you'll have the last laugh with your golfing buddies.

For this exercise, pick out an old club you no longer use regularly. A metal driver is best for three reasons:

- A metal head will not warp when immersed in water.
- A driver has the longest shaft, which displaces more water and thus receives greater resistance from it.

Swinging in a pool (or imagining that you're swinging in a pool), will encourage you to make a deliberate motion and thus help you groove the correct technique.

- A driver head, likewise, is the largest clubhead in the bag and will thus also meet increased resistance from the water.

Use a pool deep enough so that you can fill it up to your waist when you are standing in your address position. For most golfers, a 42-inch-deep pool will be adequate. Also, make sure its diameter is large enough to contain the full *width* of your swing—at least ten feet.

Once you've entered the pool and assumed the address position with your "aquatic" club, try to push the club straight back from an imaginary ball in an ultra-slow manner. Rotate your hips in a clockwise fashion, then gradually direct the club up to about waist height, where it will cut through the surface. Continue to the top of the backswing, then start down by driving your right hip downward. Your arms and the club will follow. As your hips uncoil, your arms and the club will reenter the water. Slowly continue the swing through the impact zone until you cut through the water again.

Basically, you are making the "bottom half" of your golf swing—to waist height in either direction—against the water's resistance. An excellent checkpoint is to try to mirror the driver's clubface positions at the halfway point of both the backswing and the follow-through, just as the clubhead is emerging from the water in either direction. The toe of the club should point straight up when the clubshaft is parallel to the ground on both the backswing and the follow-through. If you can ingrain these two "square" positions, you will also be ingraining a square clubface at the point of impact.

Bear in mind that you'll encounter much more resistance with the swing in the water than you will when swinging the weighted club. So, start with a smaller number of half-swings—say, ten—before trying to increase the number of repetitions.

DRILL 3: SET UP IN FRONT OF A MIRROR

A ceiling-to-floor mirror can be your best ally, short of videotape recordings, in the battle to keep your address position finely tuned. If you don't currently have a full-length mirror in your den or basement, I strongly recommend that you invest in one. You'll be able to catch any number of positional flaws before they insidiously creep into your game. Furthermore, you can watch to be sure that you are making accurate corrections to address flaws that you are already aware of.

You can and should check your address from both front and side views. From the front view, you can examine the following keys:

- **Ball Position:** With the driver, the ball should be positioned opposite your left heel (or even an inch ahead). This ensures that you make contact with your clubhead precisely at the bottom of its arc or even a shade on the upswing—a "must" for launching a powerful drive.
- **Feet Toed Out:** Both feet should be opened or toed out slightly from perpendicular. This facilitates a full and free hip turn on both the back and forward swings.
- **Head Behind Ball:** Your head should be well behind the ball to promote a solid upswing hit. If your head is directly over the ball, you will tend to contact your drives too much on the downswing and mishit the shot.

From the side view (preferably with your right or "rear" side closest to the mirror as you address the ball), you should check the following points:

- **Upper Body Bend:** You should be bent forward from your hip sockets so a 30-degree angle is formed be-

You can learn how good or bad your setup is by addressing a ball in front of a mirror.

tween your torso and thighs. This allows your arms to hang freely with ample room to swing around your body. Make sure that you maintain the normal contour of the spine.

- **Slight Knee Bend:** Remember, I advocate only a slight flex of the knees at address. Too sharp a bend is difficult to maintain throughout the swing and leads to all sorts of mishits and subsequent loss of power.
- **Hips Over Ankles:** You should be able to draw an imaginary straight vertical line from your hip joints to your ankle joints. If your hips are behind a line down to your ankles, you're crouching too much at address.
- **Right Arm Relaxed:** As you look back at the mirror, your right arm should be extended, but relaxed, and just *slightly* lower than your left arm. This means that your right arm and side are in a somewhat subservient position, where they will not take over the downswing and prematurely "throw away" the power you've built up on the backswing.

Your setup ultimately determines the motion of your swing. So, try to get yourself in front of a mirror at least once a week for an "address rehearsal" as described. It will help you keep your on-course performance in tip-top shape.

DRILL 4: BRUSH A SECOND BALL

This is a drill for specific use on the practice tee. Its purpose is to ingrain the low, slow takeaway that is essential to building a wide, powerful arc.

Tee up your ball for a normal drive. Then tee up a second ball at the same height, approximately 18 inches behind the first ball and directly along your club path. (Remember, that path is a curved, inward arc, not a straight line.) Next, assume your normal address position

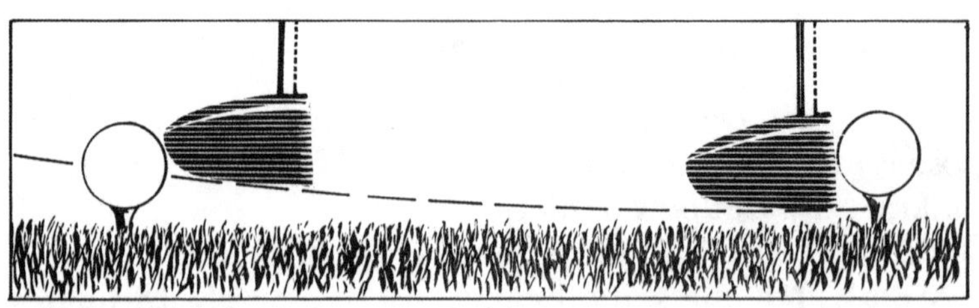

To encourage a smooth, extended takeaway, try to brush a ball off a "second" tee.

over the first ball, then employ a low, slow takeaway, making sure to brush the second ball off its tee. Retee the second ball and repeat this takeaway "brushoff" several times. Once you have the feel of it, try to make the exact same takeaway while actually hitting tee shots.

It's a good idea to go back to the checkpoint of brushing the second ball off a tee intermittently whenever you're practicing your tee shots to make certain you don't fall prey to picking up the club and shortening your arc.

DRILL 5: SWING AGAINST A WALL

This is related to the Pivot-Hip drill, as described on page 45.

Most long drivers swing the club on a relatively upright plane, with the big muscles of the back winding up as far as possible. Conversely, many short hitters swing the club on a flat plane. You can't develop your full power potential using a flat backswing plane in which your hands and arms flip the club quickly inside the target line on the backswing. That's because a "handsy" backswing prevents you from turning your upper body, cutting off a major power source.

Here's a drill to help you achieve a more upright position throughout the backswing. Take an old club, preferably a driver, and assume your address position with your back toward a wall. Assuming you're of medium height, stand with your heels three feet away from the wall. (If you're shorter than 5 feet 7 inches, stand a couple of inches farther from the wall; if over 6 feet, stand two inches closer. The reason for these adjustments is that the shorter player will naturally have a slightly more rounded swing plane; vice versa for the tall player.) Once you've positioned yourself, take your normal backswing. If your clubhead scrapes the wall before you complete the backswing, you'll know you're swinging too much around your body—that is, too *flat.*

If your backswing is too rounded, or "flat," you'll hit the wall.

If your backswing is nicely upright, and on plane too, your club will miss the wall.

To rectify the problem, return to your address position and make a low, slow takeaway, moving the clubhead straight back from the ball. When your hands have reached about hip height, allow your wrists to gradually cock the club upward, rather than turning your left wrist over so that the clubhead shoots behind you and hits the wall. Once you get the feel of that slight upward cocking motion, you'll find you can continue up to the completion of the backswing without contacting the wall. You'll be in a balanced position with your hands high, from which you can spring into a powerful downswing movement.

DRILL 6: PUT YOUR FRONT FOOT UP

A feature in the swings of all powerful drivers is that they keep their upper body behind the ball through impact. Any lateral upper body sway in the direction of the target substantially diminishes your buildup of centrifugal force and thus your clubhead speed through the impact zone. A sway also makes it difficult to square up the clubface at impact, so that you push shots to the right.

Here's a drill that will train you to keep your upper body behind the ball. When practice-swinging at home, take your normal address position, then set your front foot on an object from four to eight inches in height that will support your weight. A hard-covered briefcase is a good prop to use, particularly in an office with high ceilings. Make your driver swing, and key on pushing your right hip downward at the start of the downswing.

With your front foot set higher than normal, you'll find it's impossible to lunge forward with your upper body as you enter the hitting zone, no matter how hard you push off your right side.

You can actually hit balls with this *Front Foot Up* drill. Since you might feel a bit odd bringing a briefcase to the

Swinging with your left foot propped up helps you master the "no sway" power technique.

practice tee, you can effectively substitute a small range ball bucket turned upside down.

One final suggestion regarding this drill: At address, kick your rear knee in just a bit more than normal so that your weight is clearly on the inside of that foot. This will alleviate any inclination to sway backward, "off the ball," on the backswing.

DRILL 7: SWING INSIDE THE STAKE

Here is another drill that will prevent you from lunging to the left (toward the target) on the downswing, which is one of the most common downswing flaws among handicap golfers.

You'll need a wooden stake that extends upward to at least hip height after you've planted it in the ground. For this exercise, you can also use an old driver shaft with the clubhead removed.

Next, assume your normal address position for the driver, with the stake or clubshaft about six inches to the left of your left foot.

Now go ahead and make some practice swings, concentrating on your key downswing move, rotating your right hip in a downward drive and letting your left hip move into a supporting position. If you push the right hip down properly, your left hip will automatically move into place, laterally over the top of the left ankle, but not all the way to the stake. If you have too much lateral hip slide, you'll know it immediately because your left hip *will* hit the stake.

When working on this drill, just remember to make that downward push with the right hip counterclockwise, and you'll find that your left hip will go to the proper support position automatically.

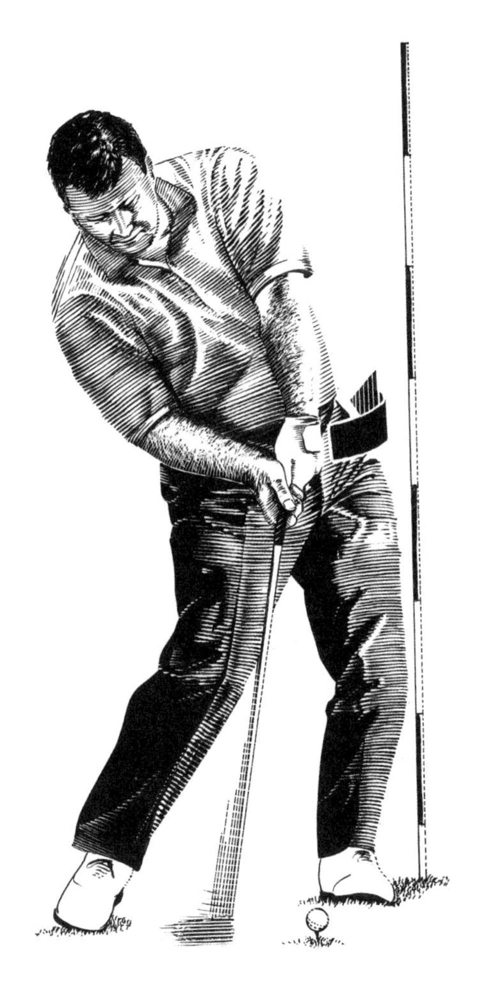

This drill encourages you to push your right hip downward at the start of the downswing and clear your left hip away from the target (and stake!) in the hitting area.

DRILL 8: SWAT THE FORWARD TEE

Are you a "quitter?" Most amateur golfers are! By that I don't mean that they give up easily or in some way lack character. What I mean is their clubheads are usually decelerating when they strike the ball. They are "quitting" on their full shots.

Trying to brush the forward tee promotes maximum clubhead acceleration.

Here's a simple drill that will provide you with the right mental image so that you can accelerate through your drives and other full shots. Tee up a ball on the practice range as you would for a normal drive. Then place a second tee in the ground, about six inches in front of the ball you plan to hit and directly along the target line. This second tee (with no ball) should be the same height as the tee with the ball.

Now go ahead and address your practice ball normally. However, instead of just hitting (or should I say "hitting at"?) that practice ball, focus on swatting the forward tee so that you either knock it out of the ground or tilt it over. Forget about the golf ball; it's merely a small impediment between you and that forward tee you want to knock over.

This adjustment in your focus may take a little getting used to, so I recommend you make at least twenty *Swat the Forward Tee* swings. By the way, you just may notice those balls that were "in the way" of the forward tee tend to fly very straight, and in a slightly lower, rising, more powerful trajectory. Why? Because now you are *accelerating* through the ball. There is no loss of the centrifugal force you've built throughout the swinging motion. You've broken out of the trap of being "impact-conscious."

Any time you find your tee shots flying a short distance and off target, go to the range and swat the "forward" tee.

DRILL 9: BEAT THE RUG

This drill requires a rope and a rug. Stretch and attach the rope between two trees or standards and place the rug over the rope. The rug should reach all the way to the ground.

Now stand 12 inches behind the rug and pretend you are hitting a golf ball through the rug. The secret of releasing the hands properly is to make the clubhead hit the rug first instead of your left arm. This is a tremendous

Freezing the ideal finish position (in practice) will help you "feel" it and swing into it on the golf course.

exercise for learning the release. Proper releasing action of the hands blended with the correct leg and torso action create the most power and effecient motion that the human body can attain.

DRILL 10: FREEZE THE FINISH

It's impossible to have a perfect, balanced, full finish if you have a poor golf swing. And while it is possible to hit good shots even though your finish is full of flaws, it doesn't happen very often. So, developing a perfect follow-through is great insurance that you're making sound, balanced moves through the impact zone—and hitting high-quality shots.

I suggest you practice making a perfect finish by taking your best swing, using a driver, then freeze the finish by holding it for one minute.

Here are the elements of a good finish that you should *freeze* into your muscle memory:

- Your weight should be almost completely on your left foot, distributed evenly on the ball and heel of the foot rather than moving onto the outside edge.
- Your right knee should be flexed and turned toward the target, while the remainder of your weight is balanced lightly on the toe of your right foot.
- Your hips, chest, and shoulders should be directly facing the target.
- Your head should also be facing the target and "up" in a natural erect position, as you follow the flight of the ball. Allow your head to swivel up to this position rather than making a forced effort to keep the head down beyond impact.
- Your left arm should be relaxed and folded back. The clubshaft should hang lightly and naturally over your left shoulder.

Hitting drives rapidly in succession eliminates body tension and stops you from thinking too much about technique.

When you can make a practice swing and *freeze the finish* that contains these elements, you'll be making a high-quality golf swing.

DRILL 11: HIT A ROW OF BALLS RAPIDLY

It's easy to get so wrapped up in the various new movements in your swing that you become tight and tense. If that happens, there's no way you can achieve your maximum power.

This final drill (which I call *Rapid Fire*) is one I advise you to employ after you have worked out the individual pieces and are ready to let the club *rip* in the hitting zone. It was shown to me by my friend Andy Franks, who is a two-time national long-drive champion.

Tee up six balls in a row on the practice tee, each about a foot apart. Set up to the first ball in correct fashion and swing without any hesitation. After watching the shot, immediately step up to the next and swing. Keep setting up and swinging with no specific thoughts about your swing mechanics. Stop when you've hit all six golf balls.

Actually, you can hit as many balls in succession as you care to in this drill. I prefer to hit only six because hitting the driver is hard physical effort, and after hitting six rapid-fire drives I'm pretty winded! If you can hit ten or twelve without panting so hard that you lose balance, then be my guest.

Something you can take from this drill to the course is the knowledge that free swinging is better than too much thinking about technique. Keep your pre-swing routine to a minimum, stay loose and in motion, and let the driver rip!

5

THE ART OF STRATEGY

Power plays and power ploys allow you to use your physical and mental strengths effectively

You know everything you need to know about the physics of hitting the golf ball hard. You have a set of drills to help you make the moves of the power golf swing second nature. Now it is time to delve into the strategies you'll need to master in order to play your most powerful and most effective game. You see, golf is not played in a vacuum where there are no distractions or pressures which can confuse you, unnerve you, or otherwise inhibit your ability to execute the power swing. Neither is a round of golf played on the practice tee, where the only obstacles in a wide expanse are the markers indicating how far your shots fly. No, you will need to make the power swing perform on the golf course. There you will encounter, among other challenges, narrow fairways (bordered by trees, water, sand, out of bounds fences) that tempt you to coax the swing and finesse the ball; windy conditions which can not only blow your shots off line, but challenge your ability to make a top-quality swing to begin with; opponents who may resort to some subtle (or not so subtle) gamesmanship in an effort to throw you off your swing; and the ebb and flow of your own confidence in your ability to hit strong, consistent golf shots. It is all of these challenges to your mind as well as your swing that make golf, in my opinion, the most demanding and testing of all sports.

One purpose of this chapter is to sharpen your visual imagery of the various types of shots you will frequently encounter. There are numerous kinds of shots that will optimize your distance in all weather conditions and on holes that bend one way or the other, have soft or hard fairways, and so on. The section entitled *Power Plays* will provide the technical and strategic processes that will help you play four of these specialty tee shots.

Also, there are situations in any round of golf, aside from the physical aspects of the shot at hand, that you must learn to overcome mentally. The second half of this chapter presents four pressure situations and the *Power Ploys* that will help you execute the mechanics when the going gets rough.

After reading this chapter, use your imagination and see if you can add some customized power plays and power ploys to specific situations you encounter frequently at your home course.

POWER PLAYS

POWER PLAY 1: *THE ROCKET DRIVE*

There are a number of circumstances in every round where you will benefit immensely from the ability to produce an extra-high, yet powerfully struck tee shot. I call this shot the *rocket drive*. Here's where it can save you yards and strokes:

The *rocket drive* is strategically the smartest shot to hit on a long par four when the wind is at your back.

With the wind behind you. The higher you can hit your tee shot (while still striking it solidly) when you've got the wind behind you, the more yardage you'll gain. Say you have a 20-mile-per-hour wind aiding you. If you hit a drive with your normal flight pattern, you'll get some extra yardage—approximately 20 yards. This gain is due almost totally to added roll. Why? When you're driving downwind, the air pushing the ball from behind knocks off most of the backspin that's been applied to the ball.(*Every* shot, even a drive, must have some degree of backspin in order to get airborne.) So, your tee shot will be getting "knocked down" as well as propelled forward by the wind. It will actually fly a little lower than normal and land on a low trajectory. So you get extra roll, but virtually no extra flight.

You need to give your downwind tee shots as much hang time as possible to take full advantage of that wind. With that same 20-mile-per-hour wind, the *rocket drive* can *carry* an extra 30 to 35 yards which, with a slight additional roll, will give you a 40-yard bonus instead of 20. And the tee shot with this flight pattern has a better chance of finding the fairway.

When the fairways are wet. Suppose your normal, well-struck tee shot on medium-speed fairways travels 230 yards, with a carry of 200 yards plus 30 yards roll. This particular day is a wet one, but your hardy foursome has decided to get the round in. However, your normal tee shot trajectory is going to give you some problems. Instead of rolling 30 yards, you'll get no more than 10 on the soggy fairways, reducing your average tee shots to 210 yards. One or two drives may even stick in the turf or "plug," yielding no roll at all.

If you're the respectable golfer who hits your drives the distances described, you'll have a very tough time scoring near your average in wet conditions. With that 20-yard loss off the tee, you'll be looking at a number of very long second shots into the par-four holes. Therefore, whether you can reach the green or not, you'll be hitting about two clubs longer than normal. The odds are, then, that you'll miss the greens with your approach shots more often than normal. Factor in that you'll miss some fairways and wind up trying to hit that longer club out of wet rough, and you can see how your score could soar. You need the *rocket drive* to play well in these conditions.

On a reachable par five or a long par four. Occasionally you'll find a par five that's short enough to allow you to get home in two with a big drive, particularly when the wind is at your back. If you can hit the rocket shot you've got a great chance to score a birdie—or eagle!

Alternatively, there may be one or two long, tough par fours on your course where you know you need a longer-than-average drive—a rocket—to get home in two.

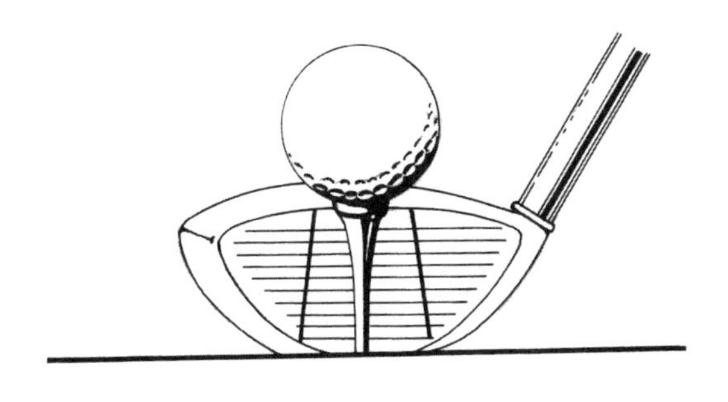

In setting up to hit a *rocket,* tee the ball extra high.

How to Play the *Rocket Drive:*

You'll always get a longer carry if you contact the ball high on the driver clubface. So your first adjustment is to tee the ball higher than normal. The ball should be sitting so that it is almost entirely above the top of the clubface.

Second, you want to meet the ball slightly more on the upswing than normal, so that you sweep the ball upward at a higher launch angle. Move the ball an inch or two forward in your stance, so that it is opposite your left instep rather than your left heel. Incidentally, your feet, knees, hips, and shoulders should be square to the target line as for a normal drive.

In the swing itself, let the takeaway be extra smooth with a full shoulder turn for good balance. On the downswing, make an extra effort to keep your upper body behind the ball until after impact, and swing your arms into a high finish.

One last tip on launching the *rocket drive:* In situations where you have a really strong wind behind you, say 25 miles per hour or more, you can actually get your maximum distance by hitting the ball on the upswing with the upper half of the clubface against the center of the golf ball. Make sure you rehearse these slight modifications mentally and mechanically before you try them out on the course.

POWER PLAY 2: *THE POWER DRAW*

The well-hit rising shot with a slight draw is the strongest shot in golf. It provides equal carry to the perfectly straight ball with several extra yards of roll, and it cuts through headwinds more effectively than a straight ball or a fade. Here are the conditions where the *power draw* is your optimum tee shot:

Around a right-to-left dogleg. Say you're facing a 400-yard par four which bends left at a fairly sharp angle about 200 yards out. Let's again assume your normal well-hit drive travels 230 yards. If you hit a straight shot up the middle, your ball will actually roll "through" the dogleg to the right side of the fairway. This means that the actual distance your two shots will need to cover is longer than the hole's measured distance. Consequently, you'll need to hit a longer club into the green.

By comparison, if you can execute the solidly hit draw shot, which is curving left with the dogleg as it descends, you'll save yards. First, the shot will be longer because of extra roll. Second, that right-to-left roll makes the shot finish in the left-center of the fairway, so you've cut vital yardage off the hole. Now you can play a shorter, more lofted iron that is far easier to hit than a long iron or fairway wood into the green.

To ride a right-to-left wind. Whenever you're driving the ball in a crosswind, you can gain valuable yards by putting the proper sidespin on the ball. When the wind is blowing strongly from right to left, the *power draw,* started well right of your target, will react almost like a shot hit with the wind at your back. The ball, spinning from right to left while the wind is pushing from the right, drives the ball "leftward" so that it lands *hot* with lots of roll back toward the center of the fairway. The *power draw* should give you at least 20 extra yards in a right-to-left crosswind, compared with a straight ball.

For extra roll to reach optimum fairway position. If you play on a hilly course, often you need a little extra distance to get your ball over a crest and down to a flat spot so that you not only have a shorter shot left but avoid a tricky downhill lie. The *power draw* can help you get "over the top" in these situations. It's also invaluable on holes where the fairway banks right to left. A great example of this is the tenth hole at Augusta National, home of The Masters. Although it's a bear of a par four at 485 yards, the tour stars can hit the *power draw* so that the ball lands and runs hard with the slope, reaching a flatter area in the left-center of the fairway—with only 160 to 175 yards left to the green.

How to Play the *Power Draw:*

You'll make the most of your adjustments for the *power draw* in your setup. First, tee the ball a fraction higher than normal. This encourages a slightly flatter swing plane, which is conducive to a right-to-left flight pattern. Next close your stance, so that your feet are aligned slightly right of where you want the ball to finish. A key point is that while your body is "closed," you should align your clubface directly where you want the ball to land. Otherwise, you're setting up to hit a straight shot a little right of your target.

Address the ball about one inch behind the left heel, to encourage contact while the clubhead is moving slightly from inside the target line with a slightly closed clubface.

Your setup alone should create the powerful drawspin you seek. Make your normal tee shot swing except for one additional point: Roll your forearms in a counterclockwise fashion as you go through the hitting zone, again to ensure that the clubface is moving from open to closed as the ball is struck.

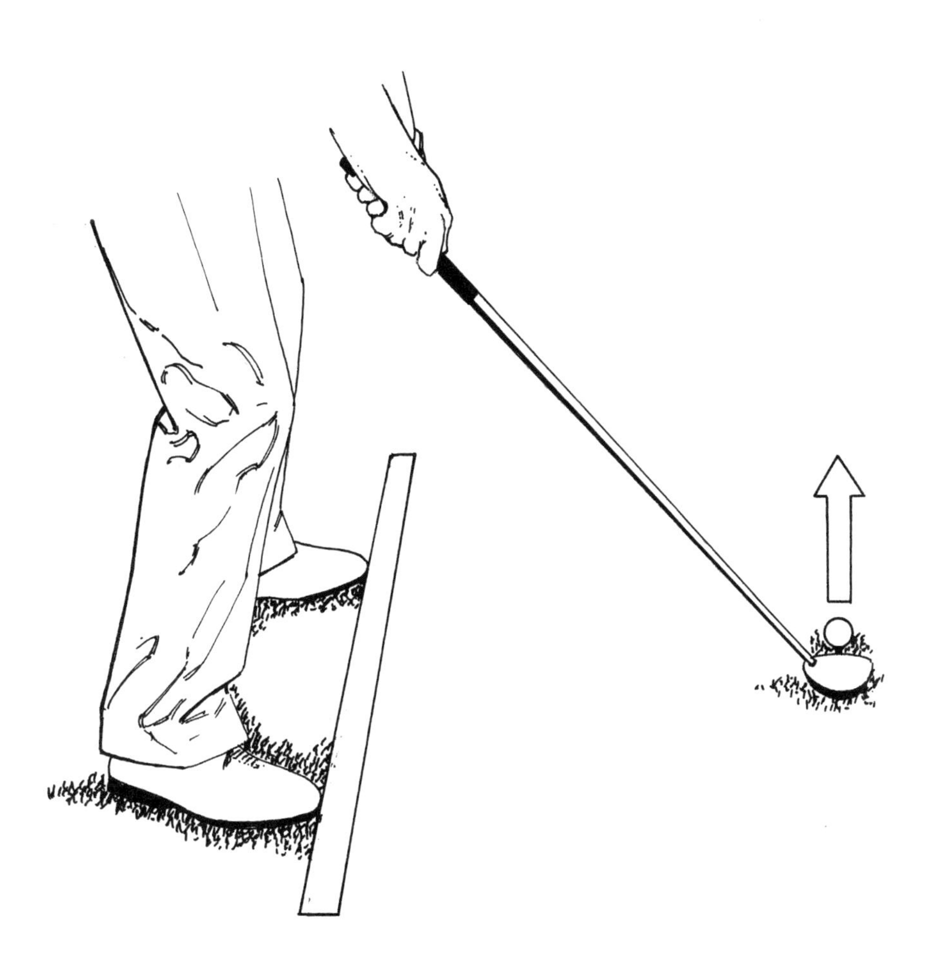

The *power-draw* setup calls for a "closed" alignment (feet and body aimed right of target) and square clubface position.

POWER PLAY 3: *THE POWER FADE*

The following situations in which the *power fade* is the most useful tee shot are basically the opposite of those discussed for the *power draw:*

Around a left-to-right dogleg. Say you're playing a hole that bends in the tee shot landing area, only this time to the right. You can save valuable yardage by hitting the *power fade* down the left center of the fairway, and letting the bend in the ball's flight match the shape of the hole. Again, you can save up to three clubs' distance on your approach shot, as opposed to making the hole longer with a straight drive that runs through the dogleg, to the left side of the fairway. In addition to saving yardage, the *power fade* lands more softly; thus it's much easier to hit a dogleg-right fairway with a ball flight that's also curving in that direction.

To ride a left-to-right wind. Putting the proper left-to-right sidespin on tee shots when the wind is blowing strongly from the left can again add some 20 yards to the shot. You must aim well left of the target to allow for the sidespin and for the strong push of the wind from the left, which drives the ball toward the fairway, again with some extra roll upon landing.

How to Play the *Power Fade:*

First, you must make some minor setup adjustments opposite to those used to hit a powerful draw.

Tee the ball lower than normal, approximately one-half inch off the ground, so that no more than one-quarter of

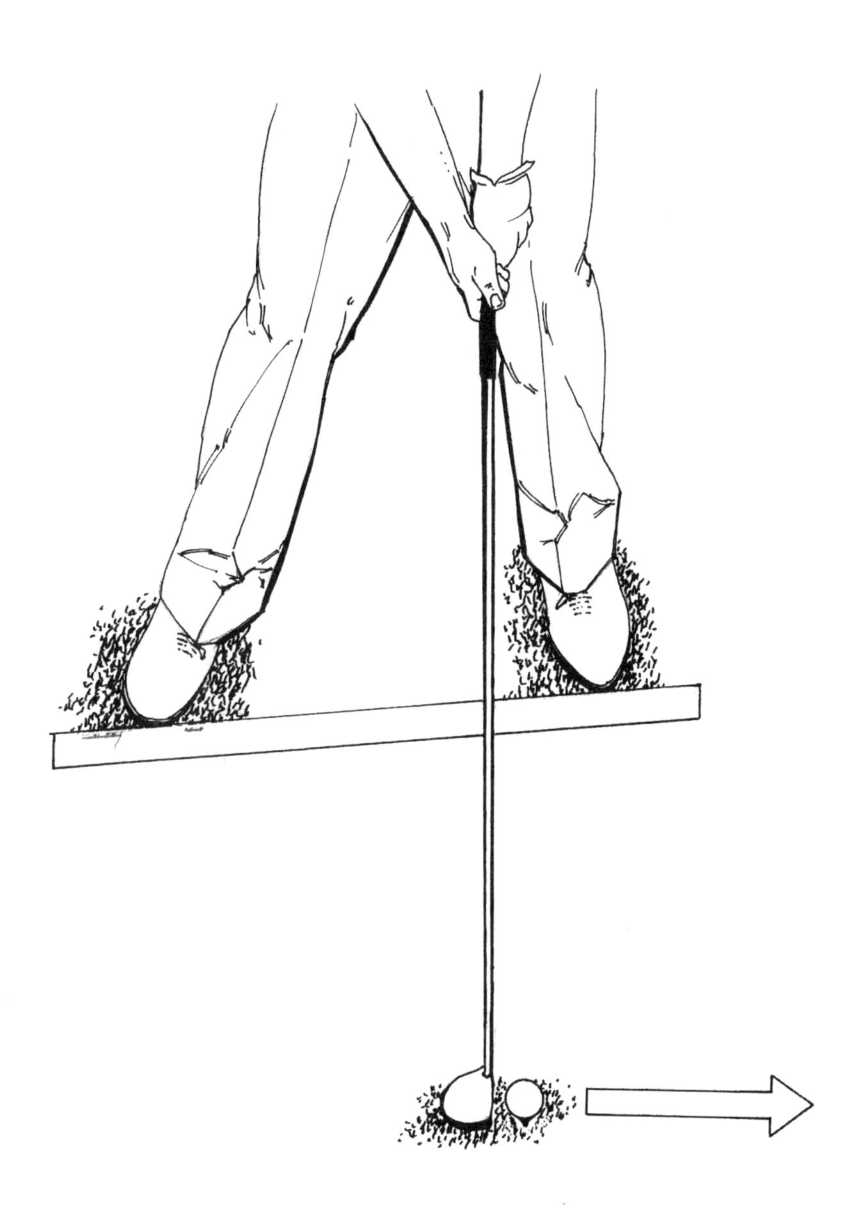

The *power-fade* setup calls for an "open" alignment (feet and body aimed left of target) and square clubface position.

the ball sits above the top of the driver's clubface. The low-teed ball automatically encourages a more upright swing, which is a technical "must" for hitting the *power fade*.

Next, align yourself so that your feet are aimed slightly left of where you want the ball to finish. If you want the ball to finish in the center of the fairway, for example, your stance should align down the left side, perhaps 15 yards left of your desired target. Again, align the clubface directly at your intended target. Thus a swing path along your body alignment will produce a trace of left-to-right sidespin, which will make the ball drive right as it loses its forward momentum. It's also helpful to play the ball one inch farther forward than normal, just in front of the left heel. This assures that the clubhead is moving along the line set up by your body rather than from inside the target line, as with the *power draw*.

Again, most of the adjustments for the *power fade* have been made before you draw the club back. Follow your basic mechanics, but place some additional emphasis on keeping the back of your left hand in control of the swing motion, in both pushing the club slowly away from the ball and pulling it through the impact zone. An especially good tip is to grip the club a bit more tightly in the fingers of your left hand. This will tend to limit your forearm rotation through the ball, ensuring that the clubface doesn't close at impact.

POWER PLAY 4: *THE BULLET DRIVE*

The *bullet drive* is aptly named because that's the way this shot flies, like a bullet shot out of a rifle. It's the mark of a fine player when he or she is able to pull this shot out of the bag on cue. Here's when the *bullet* will help you gain yardage on your opponents and the golf course:

The *bullet drive* is the perfect shot to hit when a strong wind is blowing toward you.

Into a strong wind. Maybe it only seems as though you have to hit more tee shots into the wind than downwind. Even if this really isn't true, you'll face this challenging shot often, particularly if you play on a relatively flat, open course which offers little protection from the wind. Here the *bullet drive* will really help you. For example, into a 20-mile-per-hour wind, a normally flighted drive which would have traveled 230 yards will be lucky to travel 200 yards. A well-executed *bullet* will carry nearly as far as the normal tee shot with no wind, say, 195 yards instead of 200, and will roll just as far as usual, about 30 yards, so that your 225-yard total has gained you 25 yards over your normal tee shot into this wind.

When hitting to extra-hard fairways. If your course's irrigation system is out of commission or if it's late summer and your course has baked out, take advantage via the *bullet drive.* It can easily provide you with an extra 20 yards of roll under these conditions, setting up easier short-iron approaches to par fours and possibly allowing you to get home in two on some par-five holes.

Of course, if you have a tee shot for which both of the above-stated conditions prevail—that is, it's into a strong headwind and landing on a hard fairway—then the benefit of the *bullet* is doubled. So you can see why this shot is worth learning.

How to Play the *Bullet Drive:*

More than anything else, the *bullet drive* requires great discipline, particularly into the wind, because you must resist the urge to overpower this shot. In fact, the key to the *bullet drive* lies not with any major adjustments in your backswing mechanics, but rather in swinging the club smoothly on a level or shallow downswing arc.

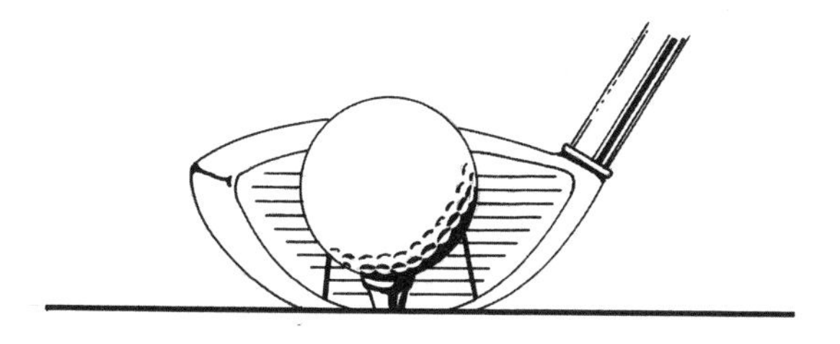

Tee the ball extra low when playing a *bullet.*

The reason is that an overly fast swing puts extra backspin on the ball. That's fine if the wind is with you or you're trying to stop an approach shot next to a tight pin position, but lots of backspin on a drive will make it upshoot or "balloon" into a wind, so that it flies much higher than normal and drops lifelessly with little or no roll. Instead, you must deliver the clubhead very *smoothly* and *levelly* into the back of the ball, as though you're trying to drive a nail into it with a hammer. This shallow delivery of the clubhead makes the ball fly off the clubface with little backspin, so it bores through the wind and lands at a shallow angle, allowing it to pick up some extra yardage on the ground.

I don't recommend any radical setup adjustments for the *bullet drive.* Tee the ball a little lower than normal, but don't tee it just above the ground as you would with an iron shot. This would encourage a downward rather than a level blow, which would result in the very "upshooter" you don't want. Likewise, it's okay to move the ball an inch or two back from your left heel, but no more, or else you'll chop down on the shot too much.

One other key adjustment is to extend your hands out into a low follow-through. Try to make your hands *chase* the ball out toward the target and you are likely to see a low *bullet* drilling through the wind and getting plenty of run after landing.

POWER PLOYS

POWER PLOY 1: *BEATING THE FIRST-TEE BUTTERFLIES*

What golfer has never experienced that sense of weightlessness in the pit of the stomach when preparing to hit his or her opening tee shot? Random thoughts race through your mind—about all the people milling around waiting for their turn to play, what your opponent thinks of your swing, will you miss the ball, and so on. As you're addressing that ball that seems so small and faraway, you've filled your mind with so many negative thoughts that you're hoping you can just get it airborne as you draw the club back.

Now I ask you, if you're setting up to hit your first tee shot of the round, while praying not to top the ball, pop it up, or knock it out of bounds, how can you possibly strike the solid, powerful tee shot that you know you are fully capable of?

It's a shame that so many golfers let the first-tee butterflies beat them, because that first drive is really such a wonderful, positive opportunity. A powerfully hit, accurate opening drive is a tremendous confidence booster and sets the tone for an entire day of solid shotmaking. All you need are some positive rather than negative images to allow you to make that good swing you've worked so hard to develop.

Recalling a solid drive you hit during a pre-round practice session will help you beat the first-tee butterflies.

Instead of dwelling on negatives, you must put your mind to work as if it's replaying a videotape recording. Block out that self-defeating awareness of bystanders, your opponents, the hazards of the hole, even your own butterflies. If you have these first tee symptoms, stop everything and take a few deep breaths. Visualize the perfect parabola of a powerful, rising, high-arcing tee shot. Make sure that your grip pressure is light to medium. Imagine that someone has just poured warm oil over the joints of your body. Fear almost always leads to excessive grip tension, which restricts a smooth flowing motion. Visualizing the desired golf shot is as important as the physical execution. Correct mental pictures must be practiced, too.

To sum up, there are times in any round of golf where you simply have to "suck it up" and play the shot boldly and fearlessly. The first tee shot is one of those times.

POWER PLOY 2: *THE POWER LAYUP*

On most golf courses, you will encounter at least one instance, perhaps two or three, where your newfound power tee shot will reach some sort of hazard. Usually it's in the form of a lake or creek that brings the fairway to an abrupt halt. Sometimes it's a more subtle restraint on your desire to launch the long ball. The fairway may dogleg sharply, so a full drive goes through the dogleg into deep rough, a fairway bunker, or even out of bounds. Thus your power drive must "thread a needle," while a shorter tee ball has much more fairway to greet it upon landing. Sometimes, it's simply a tight hole all the way, where distance is not a big factor but you *must* drive the ball in the fairway.

When you think that you could reach a hazard, or hit through the bend of a dogleg hole with a driver, a three-wood and a three-quarter swing are the perfect strategy.

If you're like most amateurs, what do you do? You go ahead and hit the driver, but decide you'll hit it easy just to make sure you don't reach the hazard and/or that you keep the ball in the tight fairway. What's the result of this strategy? More often than not, you try to coax the shot, or "steer" it, using an abrupt, choppy swing that has little or no rhythm. A poor result is almost a certainty.

Instead of trying to guide the driver in these situations, do what the pros do. Hit the *power layup* with a more lofted, weaker club. This is the ideal shot, because while you are selecting a club that will keep you short of trouble, you're still going to make an aggressive, powerful swing.

The mental key in these situations is to *be absolutely certain you can't reach the trouble with the club you select.* Say the hole is a fairly short par four, measuring 370 yards. A lake cuts off the fairway at 250 yards out. Your average drive may travel 230 yards, so you set up to hit the driver. However, you may be having a conversation with yourself that goes something like this: "I can't reach the lake—unless I really crush it, or if a gust of wind carries it farther than I expect, or if it gets a hard bounce." True, you probably won't get there, but what are your chances now of striking a solid shot? Slim to none, probably. Instead, pick the club you know won't reach the hazard, even if the wind carries it and it gets a hard bounce. Select a three-wood in this situation. Set up with the ball opposite your left heel. Then make a controlled, compact backswing, bringing the club up just short of the parallel position at the top. From there, drive the right hip downward and let the shot go as if you're trying for your best power drive. Even with a wind gust or a hard bounce, the ball shouldn't go more than 230 yards, so you're still safe. If the shot flies and bounces normally, you're about 210, or 40 yards short of the water. That's fine. The important thing is that you're much more likely to make your best swing when you know you don't have to hold back.

You'll be surprised how well you score on these tricky layup holes once you learn to attack them in this manner.

POWER PLOY 3: *THE MATCH-ON-THE-LINE TEE SHOT*

Four hours and seventeen holes after that first tee shot, you reach the final tee. The match, be it in an actual tournament or just a $2 Nassau, is either dead even or you're one up or one down. You need to play the eighteenth well to make it a successful day. Most particularly, you need a good drive to set up the hole and put the heat on your opponent. This *match-on-the-line* tee shot can be a very tough one mentally for two reasons. First, unless you're Jack Nicklaus or Greg Norman, you've probably mishit a couple of tee shots during the round, so it's natural to have some doubt that you'll catch this one perfectly. Second, on many courses the eighteenth is the most challenging hole, one that demands accuracy plus good length to get home in regulation.

How do you cope with the pressure this tee shot situation places on your shoulders? Again, a good strategy can free you up to execute the drive the way you know how to. After teeing up your ball, make a full and free *practice swing,* turning your back to the target on the backswing, making the downward push with your right hip to start the downswing, and letting your arms release freely into the classic finish position. This done, set up to the ball with the thought that you're simply going to take another practice swing. The only difference is you will hit the ball with this practice swing. Trust this approach and you'll hit some of your best tee shots when you need them most.

When the match is on the line, make a full, true-to-form practice swing; then try to repeat it when you drive.

POWER PLOY 4: *TAKE LESS CLUB UNDER PRESSURE*

You've hit the good tee shot on eighteen and you're left with a medium iron into a green that features a well-guarded pin. A good approach can win you the match and you're really pumped up. How do you handle this pressure approach shot effectively?

I firmly believe that the best way to play this shot is to take slightly less club than normal, and hit the shot *hard.*

Let's assume you have 160 yards to the pin, set on the front-left quadrant of the green, just 10 yards beyond the lip of a deep bunker. Ordinarily you hit a five-iron 160 yards with a smooth swing and 165 with a full-out swing. With a bunker to carry, it seems sensible to use a club that would put you easily over the bunker and past the pin if you hit it perfectly.

No matter how smart this sounds, I strongly suggest that when the heat is on, you play a hard six-iron shot instead of a normal five-iron. Yes, hit the six even though you'd usually have to nail it to carry the bunker. Here's why you should go with the shorter club under any similar circumstance:

- **Adrenaline flow:** Under pressure, nearly all golfers will hit their irons somewhat longer than normal. It varies with the individual, but it's safe to estimate that you'll hit the ball about ten yards farther in a spot like this. (Note: Experience is your best teacher. Go back to similar pressure approaches you've played recently. Have you airmailed the green a surprising number of times? If you answered, "Yes, by twenty yards," you may even need to drop down two clubs in these situations.)
- **Simplicity of the hard swing:** When you're under pressure it is *not* the time to try to take something "off"

When hitting an approach shot in a pressure situation, play a weaker club and hit it hard.

the shot. You don't want your mind computing the how-to's of hitting the ball extra low or fading it. Stick to the basics of making a full, solid "pass" at the ball.

- **Added backspin:** Whenever you hit an iron shot full, you apply the greatest degree of backspin to the shot. This translates to a longer carry with good stopping power once it lands, which is a big bonus when shooting to a well-guarded pin. Your chances of sticking it close with the hard six-iron are much better than by hitting a softer shot with the five-iron.

In playing the pressure approach, there is no need to adjust your address position. Just remind yourself to start the backswing with a smooth takeaway, then use your normal full swinging action while keeping your head still. Finally, follow through to a full finish. You'll find that this full-out philosophy to playing the pressure approach provides the most consistently solid end result—including a few birdies to close out the big match. Trust your instincts in these cases and you'll be rewarded.

6

THE IRON GAME

This unique, all-purpose, power-iron swing will help you recover from tricky lies

The power swing with the driver is a wide-arcing, sweeping motion which is highly desirable when launching the ball from its perch on a tee. It is also very effective in sweeping fairway woods from relatively good lies and for iron shots on the par threes, where the ball is also teed.

However, as anyone who's stepped on a golf course can attest, a substantial number of strokes must be played from imperfect fairway lies, from deep rough or other hazards in which the ball is not sitting cleanly. Power is an important prerequisite for playing many of these shots to the green; however, the power swing as you know it for the driver won't get the job done in these ticklish circumstances. For trouble shots played with the irons, the power swing will take on a slightly different form. In nearly all the trouble situations I'll describe, you will need to make a shorter but still powerful swing motion in order to get the club cleanly on the ball. Generally, these shots will require you to make the following adjustments:

- A quicker wrist break in your takeaway.
- A more upright swing plane.
- A substantially narrower swing arc than with the driver. (The swing arc is naturally narrower as the clubs get shorter. However, when I say your swing arc will be narrower, it will also be due to the sharper wrist break you will be employing.)
- An emphasis on making a faster downswing pivot, which increases arms-hands-club speed.

Mind you, in most of the situations I'm about to describe, you will need a brisk, powerful action to make the shot work. What I will refer to as my "all-purpose-recovery-power-swing" is merely a different application of power to the ball than you apply with the driver.

The first essential in playing these power-iron recoveries is to recognize the situations that call for them, so you'll know when and how to make the proper subtle adjustments in your technique. In this chapter I will break down these recoveries into two categories: power shots played with the middle irons (the four, five, and six), and aggressive partial shots played with the pitching irons.

FOUR "POWER" SHOTS WITH THE MEDIUM IRONS

---

1. BALL IN MEDIUM-TO-DEEP ROUGH

This is the most common situation where you'll need to employ the power-iron swing. You've pulled or pushed your tee shot into moderately heavy rough, and are middle-iron distance to the green.

The first thing you need to do is to carefully assess the severity of your lie. Many times when the rough is not particularly thick or high, it will offer little resistance to the clubhead through the impact zone, so that you hit a "flyer." In these cases the ball jumps off the clubface more quickly, but because some grass inevitably intervenes between the clubface and the ball, there's less backspin than normal. The ball thus runs more upon landing. A flyer shot actually travels one to two clubs—about 10 to 20 yards—farther than normal.

Watch out for lies where you might consider the rough to be medium in depth, but the grass has been run over continually by golf carts, so that it's leaning strongly toward the hole. Here, also, you'll encounter little resistance from the grass and the ball will fly.

These exceptions excluded, you will normally need a forceful swing to send the ball medium-iron distance from the rough. If you play a course which has bent-grass rough, I would define medium to fairly heavy rough as three to five inches deep, with the grass neither lying with nor strongly against you. If the rough is Bermuda, then a two-and-one-half- or three-and-one-half-inch depth would be considered medium rough, because Bermuda grass is a lot thicker than bent. It will resist the drive of the clubhead through the ball much more stubbornly.

In playing this shot, your object is to allow as little grass between the club and the ball as possible. This means that the clubhead must descend on the ball at a sharper angle than normal. Your first adjustment, then, is to move the ball back in your stance, so that it's slightly back of center. In addition, your stance should be a trifle narrower than for a shot from the fairway to encourage a very upright swing. To further promote a steep back-and-through swing that will allow you to hit the ball more cleanly at impact (with less grass coming between clubhead and ball), stand two inches closer to the ball.

When playing a medium-iron shot from the rough, raise the club well above the ground to promote a sharp, downward hit.

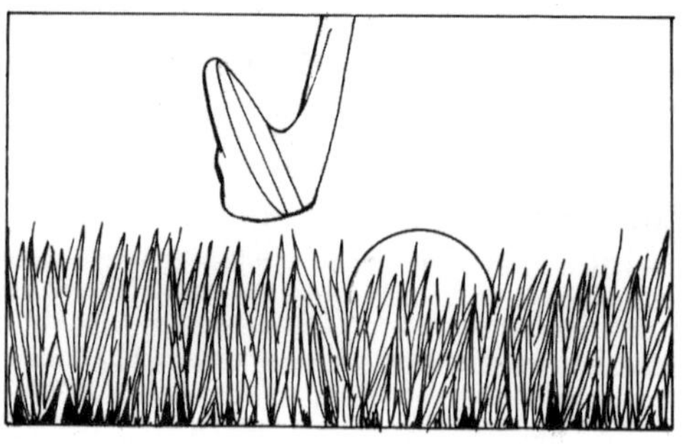

Last, grip the club more firmly than normal to counteract the greater resistance you'll encounter. While I judge my grip pressure as five on a scale from one to ten for tee shots, I recommend turning the pressure up to nine for shots from the rough.

A useful tip in playing these shots is to hover the club slightly above the ball at address rather than directly behind it. First, this hovering action acts as insurance that you won't jostle the grass directly behind the ball (before you swing), causing it to move, so that you incur a penalty stroke. Second, it encourages you to drive the clubhead downward through impact.

Going back, make a compact three-quarter swing.

To start the downswing, push your right hip downward more forcefully. This will increase the force of your pivot and with that enable you to accelerate the club more powerfully through the impact zone with your hands leading the club. The force of the hit will easily extract the ball from the rough and send it flying toward the target.

Because, in hitting this shot, the hands lead the club downward, the clubface will be somewhat "de-lofted" at impact, causing the ball to shoot out at a lower angle; a six-iron shot, for example, will come out like a five. The ball will run a little more than usual upon landing, so allow for it if there is no bunker in front of the pin. If there is, then the smart play is to aim for the widest area, or "fat," of the green, to allow for the larger margin of error that playing from rough demands.

One final caution: If you are playing from a poor lie in heavy, clinging rough that's six inches deep or more, then forget the green. Take your medicine and select the loft you need to chop the ball back into play, whether it's a nine-iron, pitching wedge, or even the sand wedge. Use the same setup and swing principles and you'll advance the ball the maximum yardage possible.

2. THE MID-IRON CLOVER SHOT

Quite often you'll find your tee shot has come to rest in a patch of clover, in either the rough or the fairway. A ball lying in clover looks innocuous enough, and many golfers will not recognize that this shot must receive special treatment. However, it must, because those bright green clover leaves retain a great deal of moisture, much more than ordinary grass blades do. Also, the ball tends to sit "down" in clover. Therefore, if the clubhead comes into the ball in a normal sweeping action, the clover leaves smashed between clubhead and ball release a surprising amount of moisture. The clubface gets almost no grip on the ball and you get that uncontrolled knuckleball flight—the classic flyer.

To recover from this lie, you need to use a technique in which the clubhead of a middle iron descends on the ball at an extra-steep angle, so you get as little clover as possible between clubface and ball. In setting up, take a very narrow stance and set your hands as many as three to four inches ahead of the ball. The hands-ahead position will set you up to come into the ball from a steep angle and make a hard hit, so grip pretty firmly—a seven on my one-to-ten scale.

Since you want to fully ensure a narrow swinging arc, start the club back with an earlier-than-normal wrist cock. Then, as the clubhead reaches waist height, reach for a high hands position at the top of your swing.

Trigger the downswing by driving your legs toward the target, and then pull the club down sharply into the back of the ball. Because of the downward thrust, the clubface might close a hair at impact, causing the ball to pop out nicely but fly a little bit from right to left. So, allow for this when setting up.

Despite these instructions, it's difficult to completely

You'll play a good recovery shot from clover if you swing back on a steep plane.

eliminate the flyer effect of clover. Consequently, it's strategically intelligent to select one club less than you would from a nice tight lie in the fairway. If the hole is on the green's top tier, plan to land the ball toward the front of the green, since the ball will release a bit more than usual upon landing.

3. THE MIDDLE IRON FROM HARDPAN

This shot scares many golfers, but the truth is that the middle-iron shot from hardpan is much easier to control than shots from rough or clover. Why? Because there is no grass to intervene between the clubface and the ball at impact. You can put the clubface cleanly on the ball and impart plenty of spin on it. Therefore you can not only stop the ball more quickly, you can also draw or fade the shot if the pin placement so requires.

The reason many amateurs get psyched out by hardpan lies is that they sense there is no cushion beneath the ball (as with a normal fairway lie), and therefore they can't get away with a shot that's hit a shade heavy, or "fat." Well, the goal on all iron shots is to strike the ball with a descending blow; you have to have faith that you can do so in a situation such as this, where admittedly there is a smaller margin for error than when hitting off manicured fairway grass. Some minor adjustments in the setup will encourage that descending blow and take the unnecessary fear away from what is truly an opportunity to get the ball close to the hole.

The swing arc for this hardpan shot needs to be only slightly steeper than for a good fairway lie, since there's no worry about grass getting caught between club and ball. You do, however, want a little extra insurance that you'll hit the ball cleanly. To accomplish this goal, address the ball just one inch back from a line opposite your left heel, with your hands slightly ahead of the ball. Assume a square

If your ball lies on hardpan, toe the clubface in at address to compensate for it opening at impact.

stance of normal width for a middle-iron shot, with your heels not quite shoulder-width apart. Now, the most important setup key or swing "hook": Toe the clubface in a bit so that it's just slightly closed to the target line as you sole the clubhead behind the ball. This will compensate for the tendency of the clubface to open upon contact with the hard ground. Choke down on the club about one inch for extra control, and grip only a little more firmly than normal.

I recommend that you extend the club on the takeaway along the target line a little longer than on the previous two shots. Begin to cock your wrists upward only after your hands have passed your right knee. Then swing your arms up to the three-quarter position while your lower body remains passive.

On the downswing, concentrate on trying to straighten your right arm in the hitting area. Keep your head steady and look intently at the top of the ball to ensure powerful "ball-first" contact.

When struck properly, this shot will rise gently to its apex and land softly. Therefore, as with the shots hit from rough or clover, you can attack the flag, even if it is fairly well protected. If you feel confident in your swing, as you should, go for the "stick."

Keep in mind that the shot from hardpan will travel a shade shorter than normal because you've choked down on the grip slightly, and the club's arc is a little narrower than normal. Usually you'll be better off going with a stronger, less-lofted club—say, a four-iron instead of a five.

4. THE QUICK-STOPPING MIDDLE IRON

Here's a situation in which the lie of the ball doesn't present the problem; rather, the position of the flag does. You've hit a really nice drive down the right-center of the

Good hand action is a technical "must" if your goal is to hit a quick-stopping iron into a green.

fairway which leaves you about a five-iron distance from the pin. The problem is that the pin is tucked just 15 feet behind a deep bunker guarding the right front of the green.

You may opt to play safe to the middle of the green, but since your lie is perfect you can put it close if you know how to generate power and play the extra-quick-stopping shot. Here's how.

The most important setup key is to assume a slightly open stance by pulling your left foot a tad back from the target line while keeping your clubface square. This will automatically give you an out-to-in swing path that puts a trace of left-to-right spin on the ball for a very soft landing.

On the backswing, cock your wrists a little early, and continue swinging on a fairly upright plane with your arms controlling the movement. A three-quarter position at the top is perfect for this shot.

Start down by pulling hard with both hands. To ensure that you contact the ball flush and hit a quick-stopping, "biting" shot, make a low, extended finish, with your arms and the clubshaft pointing toward the target.

Since the ball is loaded with backspin it will rise quickly near the end of its trajectory and drop to the green at a steep angle. If the shot has been executed correctly, the ball will take one short hop, then stop dead.

The quick-stopping middle iron is a great shot to have in your bag, and it's a lot of fun to play. Two points of caution, however. First, with your compact swing and the slight fading action on the ball, the shot will fly about a half-club or five yards shorter than average. Second, since a high percentage of amateur players use a "solid" or "one-piece" ball, it's only fair to mention that no matter how crisply you strike this shot, it will not bite as fast as it will if you are playing a wound or "two-piece" balata ball. Allow for this when planning the shot.

POWER RECOVERIES WITH THE PITCHING IRONS

1. THE PITCH SHOT FROM A DIVOT

You hit the ball in the fairway, within nine-iron or pitching-wedge distance of the flag. Then, when you walk to it from the teeing area, you see the ball is lying in a divot hole!

Most club golfers tense up in this situation and don't give themselves a chance to execute the shot properly. You can recover, though, as long as you make the proper adjustments.

The fatal error most players make here is to try to scoop the ball out of the divot hole. It's almost impossible to do anything but top the shot using this approach. Instead, you must hit with an exaggerated descending blow. To help you do this, move the ball well back in your stance, just behind its center. Because your hands are ahead of the ball, the clubface will now point more toward the ground in a "hooded" position, effectively taking loft off the club.

Create a steep backswing arc by cocking your wrists almost immediately on the takeaway, then swinging your hands and arms almost straight up. From the top, you should utilize your lower body fully. However, instead of uncoiling your hips in a counterclockwise direction, which creates a sweeping action, start down by driving your knees and hips laterally at the target. This will add to the steepness of your downward arc as you pull the club sharply through impact.

You should trust the club to lift the ball from the divot hole and land the ball with good backspin. Don't help it up. However, play a higher-lofted club (a pitching wedge,

Driving your legs toward the target on the downswing will help you dig the ball out of a divot hole.

for instance, instead of a nine-iron) to compensate for the ball-back address position, which reduces the club's normal loft.

Work on this shot next time you're on the practice tee (there are plenty of divot holes out there). You'll quickly realize this shot is not as tough as it looks.

2. BALL LYING IN EDGE OF GREENSIDE WATER HAZARD

You watch forlornly as your approach shot misses the green, then trickles into a greenside water hazard. Before you take an "automatic" penalty stroke or concede the hole, take a close look at the situation. Is any part of the ball showing above the water's surface? If it is, and you can get reasonable footing, you can hit this shot out onto the green—maybe even close to the hole for a "career" par.

Because you will literally *splash* the ball out, play this shot with a sand wedge. Any other club features too sharp a leading edge and tends to slice too deeply behind the ball. And, oh yes, slip on rain pants if you have them in your golf bag.

Address the ball with an open stance and the ball forward, off your left instep. Hover your sand wedge above and behind the ball with an open clubface, which brings the flange of the club more into play. The closer you are to the hole, the more you should open the clubface. Make certain the club doesn't touch the water at address or in swinging back, or else you'll incur a penalty stroke.

You should execute this shot as if your ball is in sand rather than water. Swing the club outside the target line, but slightly farther back than you would for a sand shot of the same length. Then aim for a spot two inches behind the ball and swing down aggressively with your hands and

Opening the clubface helps you "splash" the ball out of water.

arms, while keeping your head and body still. The ball should pop up out of a fountain of water and hopefully land close enough to the hole for a reasonable chance at a great par save.

3. THE HALF-SAND, HALF-GRASS PITCH

Your ball has come to rest on the edge of a bunker, lying in a mixture of sand and grass. You need to loft the ball over the bunker's high front lip and stop it rather quickly to finish close to the hole. I'll admit it, this is a tough shot, but let me show you the right technique to play it successfully.

In playing this shot, don't do what high-handicap players do: make a half-hearted attempt to pick the ball clean from the half-sand, half-grass lie. The odds are great that you'll mishit the shot using this approach. A skulled shot clear across the green or a fat shot into the trap right in front of you are the most likely results.

By attacking the shot aggressively, you'll have a much better chance of getting within one-putt range. First, select a pitching wedge. Then, in setting up, purposely stoop over to promote a steep plane of swing. Position yourself so that the ball is forward in your stance, off the left heel. Your weight should, however, favor your right side, so keep your head tilted back slightly to facilitate this. To further promote height, open the clubface of the pitching wedge just slightly. Take aim for a spot one inch behind the ball.

The swinging action is dominated by your arms, with little body turn, since maintaining balance is paramount. The correct length of swing requires practice, but the amount of force should be slightly more than for a normal bunker shot of the same length. Throughout the swing,

Making a fluid armswing, while keeping the lower body "quiet," is the secret to recovering from a half-grass, half-sand lie.

keep your eyes riveted on that spot just behind the ball that you wish to contact.

From the top, the shoulders, arms, wrists, and hands rotate in an abbreviated pivot. This shot provides height, not length. The blade of the pitching wedge will cut into the turf and under the ball (whereas the sand wedge would wrongly bounce off the ground and hit the top of the ball). Strive for a normal follow-through, with your body facing the target—good insurance against "quitting" at impact and mishitting the shot into the sand trap. The ball should fly softly and run only a short distance upon landing. Remember: Be aggressive and strike sharply behind the ball rather than trying to pick it clean, and the odds for success are with you.

4. THE PITCH FROM DEEP ROUGH

If you've missed the green and your ball has come to rest in heavy rough, it pays to know how to hit this "touch" shot, particularly if there's a bunker between you and the hole.

First, inspect the lie. If the ball is down in deep rough and there's no cushion under it, your main objective is to dig the ball out and just get it safely on the green. In this case, use a sand wedge and assume a square stance with the ball midway between your feet. Pick the club straight up with your arms and pull the clubhead down sharply as you concentrate on the back of the ball. It will come out a little lower than with your normal pitch and will run a bit more also, since the long grass won't allow you to put much spin on the ball. But this is the smartest play when the lie is really poor.

If the ball's in deep rough but there is some cushion underneath it, you have the green light for the "soft pitch." Your goal here is to slide the clubface under the ball to

The number-one downswing "hook," when playing a wedge out of a cushioned lie in deep rough, is to keep your head behind the ball in the hitting area.

throw it high in the air. To accomplish this, make the following setup adjustments: Move the ball forward, in an exaggerated open stance, opposite your left instep; open the face of your sand wedge about 20 degrees; set your weight more on your right side than usual.

Keep your grip pressure lighter than normal as you settle into the shot, since a light grip will help you produce the loose, almost lazy swing action you need here. Your right hand will control the backswing, cocking the club up rather quickly away from the ball. Practice will determine how far back to swing for the required distance, but generally, you should make a slightly longer, wristier backswing than you would for a basic pitch, always keeping your rhythm smooth.

The downswing is also a right-hand-dominated move. Aim for a spot about one and one-half inches behind the ball, rather than the ball itself. Uncock your right wrist freely, coming down so the clubhead moves in a scooping motion, while at the same time keeping your head and your weight well behind the ball. Your open-faced sand wedge will slide through the grass and under the ball, forcing it to come out very softly and land on the green with very little run.

A RECOVERY SHOT THAT'S NEITHER "FISH NOR FOWL"

We've discussed a number of middle-iron-distance specialty shots to be hit from problem lies and, also, recovery shots from closer in with your pitching clubs. Here's a recovery shot that I consider neither fish nor fowl, because it's a very short stroke, yet it's played with a five-iron.

Every golfer has experienced that almost-but-not-quite approach shot which falls short of the target and "plugs" deep in the sand, under the bunker lip. You figure there's no way to get it out of there with one swing. Instead of giving up, try this: Take your five-iron and turn it upside down, so that the toe of the club is addressing a spot directly behind the ball. What you will do is drive the toe of the club into the sand, so that it pops the ball up and onto the green—believe it or not! You will need a short decisive chopping motion (plus a little nerve) to make this unusual shot work. Address the ball with your hands well ahead of it, so the toe of the club is well-positioned to drive into the sand behind and then under the ball, rather than into the ball itself. Grip down on the shaft to enhance control.

As you concentrate on a spot in the sand just behind the buried ball, make a straight-up half swing using your hands. Then drive the toe of the club sharply into the sand, right at the base of the ball, while keeping your head and body "quiet."

The toe of the club will literally stick in the sand, but the ball will pop up over the bunker's lip and trickle onto the green.

This shot works because you are applying all the force of the clubhead to one small area of sand. To generate the necessary high degree of force needed to extract the ball from the "plug," pull down on the club extra hard the split second you complete the backswing.

Practice this unique shot a few times to get the feel of the necessary short chopping motion, and to gain confidence in it. Then you'll have a secret weapon handy whenever that "impossible" buried bunker lie confronts you.

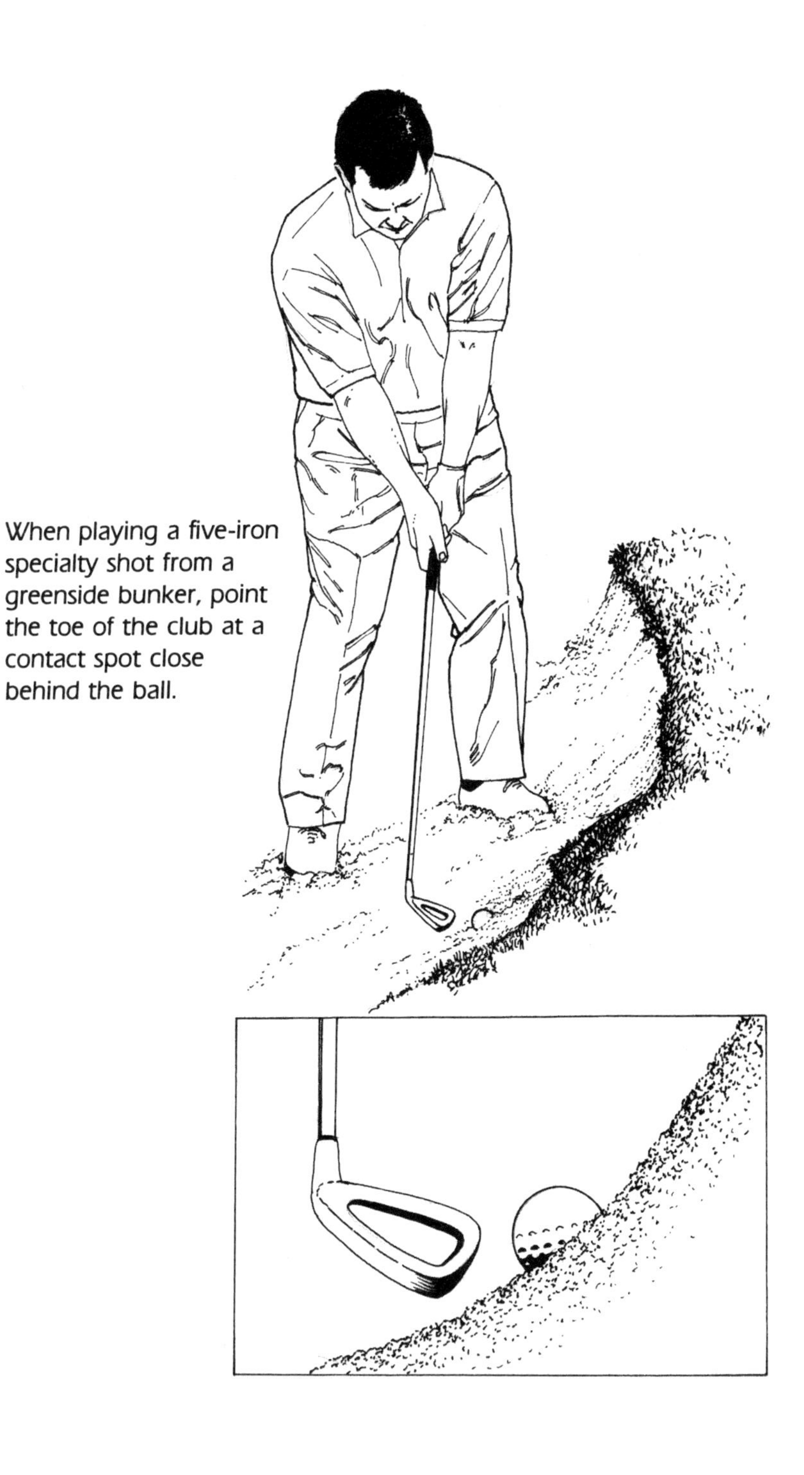

When playing a five-iron specialty shot from a greenside bunker, point the toe of the club at a contact spot close behind the ball.

Ken Lewis

7

THE RIGHT EQUIPMENT

A made-to-measure driver will definitely improve your prowess off the tee

Have you been hoping that someday you will happen across that one *perfect* driver that provides you with the finest possible combination of length and accuracy, given your swing characteristics? Welcome to the club—a very large club that includes virtually everyone who plays the game of golf seriously. And there is a very good reason to make a diligent search for that perfect driver, since the driver may just be *the* most important club in your bag.

The importance of being a competent and confident driver of the ball—and you have to have the right driver to be competent and confident off the tee—goes far beyond the actual number of strokes you may make with the club during each round. There are usually fourteen driving holes on a regulation golf course (excluding par threes). Of the fourteen driving holes, you might hit the driver every time, or there may be one or two holes whose configuration is such that you decide to hit a three-wood or long iron instead. Be that as it may, for the average golfer who shoots around 90, driver shots represent about 15 percent of all shots played.

I believe, however, that the total significance of tee shots goes far beyond 15 percent of the game of golf. That's because the drive *affects every other shot you play on the hole.* If you hit a long drive, it means your approach shot will be made with a shorter iron, and the odds of hitting the green and getting close to the hole get better. If that long drive has found the fairway, you're also playing from a good lie, and the odds of a successful approach shot improve that much more.

Conversely, if you're driving poorly, everything else becomes a struggle. A short drive, even if it's in the fairway, leaves you straining to reach the green with a long iron or fairway wood. The odds of hitting greens with the long clubs get substantially worse, even for better players. And sometimes, you won't be able to reach the green at all.

Of course, if you're hitting your drives both short *and* crooked, you have the worst of both worlds. Not only will you not hit many greens in regulation, but you've also opened the door for those demoralizing sevens and eights that wreck your scorecard. And almost any time you suffer a disastrous hole, you can look back and realize that the poor score can be traced to a poor tee shot.

While I know all this sounds negative, the point I'm trying to make is that those fourteen drives you hit control the outcome of your round. I am convinced that if you are a middle- to high-handicap player, by developing a sound, competent driving game, you can easily cut as many as eight to ten strokes off your score.

Believe me, your perspective on the game of golf will be a heck of a lot better when you're wedge distance from the pin, in the fairway.

I have talked about the setup and swing mechanics that will lead you toward better driving. Now it's time to help you find the right driver to complete the package. It is especially important to consider your equipment after you've made your swing adjustments second nature. That's because once you have done so, a driver whose specifications might have been acceptable with your old swing is now obsolete. As your mechanics improve, so must your selection of equipment.

LEARN FROM MY TRIALS AND TRIBULATIONS

For someone like myself, whose living and reputation are based on my standing as the world's *number-one long drive authority,* the stakes involved in finding the best possible driver are, if you don't mind my saying so, a little higher than they may be for you. Over the past decade, I have tested hundreds of drivers. There are so many significant variables—shaft material, shaft stiffness, grip size, swingweight, and clubhead material are just a few. Now consider that each of these club makeup factors may offer innumerable choices, just within that one area. For example, there are dozens of shaft flexes available today, gradations within the straightforward *regular, stiff,* or *extra stiff* labels of years past. If you matched up every possible shaft flex with every possible loft angle with every possible size of head, and so on, you would spend the rest of your life trying out drivers.

My goal here is to simplify this intimidating and confusing process by explaining how I determined the driver characteristics that were right for me. Then, based upon my own trials, I will make some suggestions that will at least point you in the right direction. This will enable you to greatly narrow your search parameters. Then you can fine-tune your way to finding the perfect driver, rather than blindly trying out drivers with all kinds of varying characteristics.

I can't state this too strongly: Don't just order a duplicate of what your club champ uses, or what Jack Nicklaus uses, or what I use. Learn what makes sense for you, based on your new improved driver swing.

Now let's discuss eleven components of club design for the driver, starting with those involving the "business end" of the club, then working our way up to the shaft, the grip, and the final overall component, swingweight.

1. CLUBHEAD MATERIAL

Does it seem so long ago that the driver and the other "wood" clubs were always made out of wood and wood alone? You can't tell it by looking through your foursome's golf bags or by observing the merchandise that's stocked in your pro shop. Wood drivers still make up a fair percentage of the market, to be sure, but there are so many other offerings—among them metal, graphite, carbon graphite, and thermoplastic. Of course, the explosion in the use of metal since the early '80s is the dominant story in the development of "wood" clubheads. Well over half of all driver clubheads are now constructed of metal as opposed to wood and all other materials combined.

There are several major differences in the design of a metal and a wood-headed driver, and some important differences in the ball flights they provide. A wooden driver head, of course, is a solid block of natural persimmon or a block of laminated layers of wood, which is of virtually equal density throughout the clubhead. A metal head, meanwhile, is actually hollow in the center, or "perimeter-weighted." This is because metal is much heavier than wood; it's impractical to manufacture a solid metal head of standard size, since it would weigh far too much.

We have learned in recent years that perimeter-weighted drivers (in fact, all perimeter-weighted clubs) tend to be more forgiving of off-center hits. Because there is more mass behind the ball with a perimeter-weighted metal driver, when it is struck somewhere away from the sweet spot the ball tends to fly a little straighter and a little closer to solid-hit distance. Or to put it another way, your bad drives turn out a little better with metal.

The ball also tends to fly a little straighter with metal because a metal clubface puts less spin on the ball than wood does. It's harder to hit a really severe hook or slice with a metal driver. Last, because there's slightly less spin, you'll usually get a bit more roll as a bonus.

Considering all these facts, I recently made a permanent switch to a metal driver, the "Big Bertha" model made by Callaway Golf. (See table for my complete driver specifications.)

Your Choice

If you have a wood-headed driver that you have developed great confidence in and which you hit consistently solidly, I wouldn't argue with you for sticking with it. But for any player who does not connect with the sweet spot almost all the time, the advantages of a perimeter-weighted club are virtually overwhelming. If you're ready for a new driver, start your search with metal-headed clubs.

2. CLUBHEAD SIZE AND DESIGN

To some degree, the size and design of the driver clubhead are related to the clubhead material you select. Wood drivers have always offered a great degree of flexibility in terms of size and shape of clubhead. In their early days, metal driver heads were somewhat limited as to overall possible head size because of the difficulty in keeping the total weight of a steel head within normal limits. Advances in technology in the past few years, however, have allowed manufacturers to offer a wide range of sizes and shapes of metal heads. So for all intents and purposes, you can now find whatever type head is best for you, in any material.

As a rule, long hitters prefer to use drivers with larger heads. There are two reasons for this. First, a big-headed driver looks good when you address the ball with it. Size breeds confidence, which is an all-important factor. Second, a large head has a higher center of gravity than a small one, because the clubface is deeper from top to bottom. A power hitter needs this deeper clubface so that the clubhead's center of mass meets the back of the ball squarely, driving the ball forward with a boring flight pattern for maximum distance. If a strong player uses a driver with the exact same loft as usual but with a shallower clubface, the center of mass will contact the ball slightly below its equator. The ball will then leave the clubface at a much higher launch angle, and the player will lose distance.

As you can imagine, I like a driver with a big head both for the confidence factor and for a more driving ball flight. The Callaway Big Bertha I use (see illustration) has one of the largest clubfaces and deepest heads (from front to back) in the industry. Another advantage of this head, and an advantage that metal technology has over wood, is that there is very little metal used in the hosel or "neck" area of the club. A wooden hosel area is larger by necessity to withstand stress and keep the wooden head from eventually cracking. With metal, all the head weight can be placed more effectively behind the ball.

Your Choice

You have to be realistic. A big, "bomber" head is not for you if you generate a swing speed below 80 miles per hour with the driver. If the head is too big for your swing speed,

Choosing a driver with a big "head" will boost your confidence.

you'll hit shots that nosedive in flight early. This is why many senior golfers find they obtain their optimum flight with a shallow-faced driver (less than one and one-half inches in depth) or perhaps even a two-wood. Whatever your swing speed at impact, you should go with the biggest head you can, to aid your confidence, without getting so big and deep you feel you have to help the ball into the air.

3. CLUBFACE LOFT

This is one area of driver design in which a wealth of options awaits you, particularly with metal drivers. Once you've found the clubhead design you like, you can choose among several different loft angles, one of which will be right for you.

After much experimentation, I have settled on a driver with eight degrees of loft. This is a fairly low loft angle, but the longer a hitter you are, the lower the loft you can and should play with. And I might add, eight degrees of loft with a metal driver is not the lowest available. So you see, even I do not automatically select the strongest possible specifications.

One interesting point to keep in mind regarding loft is that, all other factors being equal, metal drivers hit the ball approximately one degree higher than wood drivers. Without becoming too technical, research has determined that this is so because the center of gravity in metal heads is farther back than in wood heads. At impact, centrifugal force gives the metal clubhead a trifle more forward "kick," adding slightly to its effective loft at impact. What this means is that, if eleven degrees of loft with a wood driver is right for you, then a metal driver with ten degrees of loft will provide approximately the same trajectory.

Your Choice

Select a driver loft you can get airborne comfortably. Of course, the more clubhead speed you generate, the lower the loft you should play with. Two other points to consider: If you draw the ball consistently, you'll benefit from a bit of extra loft since your clubface is a shade closed through impact. Conversely, if you hit a fade, a little less loft will help you.

Also consider the prevailing conditions you play under. If your home course is hilly with soft, plush conditions, you can "buy" a higher carry by going with one more degree of loft. If you play on a flat course that's open to the wind, with dry, hard fairways, go with a lower loft for a wind-fighting trajectory and added roll.

4. CLUBFACE ANGLE

You might assume that driver clubfaces are always manufactured to lie "square" to the target line. This is definitely not always the case. Some manufacturers' clubs tend to lie "open" to the target line, while other designs on the market lie "closed." Some companies will offer driver lines with all three options (open, square, or closed) available.

If you play golf with a wood driver, whether you know it or not, you're probably playing with a clubface angled slightly *open* to the target line. Most wood drivers are angled, on average, about two degrees open to the target line. This is done for a good reason. Wood drivers, because of certain specifics of their clubhead design, tend to close a bit through the impact zone. The slightly open clubface is intended to offset this tendency.

Virtually all metal clubhead designs do not force them to close through impact; thus, most manufacturers design their metal drivers to sit square at address. I personally find that a square clubface suits me fine. However, many manufacturers now offer slightly open or closed clubfaces to offset the swing flaws of the golfing public.

Your Choice

An open-faced driver can certainly help if you consistently hook the ball; a closed-faced driver will assist you in straightening out a chronic slice. While I have no objection to your using an open or closed clubface angle, keep in mind that either is a "Band-Aid" for one or more swing flaws. I'd much rather see you learn to employ sound swing mechanics to help you deliver the clubhead squarely to the ball as it moves directly down the target line. Then go with a square-faced driver.

5. SHAFT LENGTH

Generally the longer the club, the greater the speed you will generate in the clubhead through the impact zone. Futhermore, the greater the clubhead speed, the farther you will hit the ball. So, why don't we all play with driver shafts that are, say, eight feet long?

The reason, of course, is that you have to deliver the clubhead *accurately* as well as with maximum speed. And there is a limit to how long a club any golfer can swing with accuracy.

The generally accepted "standard" driver length is 43½ inches (some manufacturers call 43 inches their "standard" length). I have experimented with many shaft lengths in my search for distance, some fairly outrageous (although I've never used a shaft as long as the 53 inches that I've seen some of my competitors use in long-driving competitions). I have settled on a driver length of 44 inches, just one-half inch longer than standard. I've found that this length gives me the best combination of clubhead speed and control. And actually, I choke down on the club about one-half inch, for reasons of personal feel and comfort.

Your Choice

It might pay to spend some time on the practice tee with a longer-shafted driver. A long driver will help you generate extra clubhead speed. Furthermore, it automatically gives you a flatter swing plane; in turn, that more rounded plane angle will yield a long-running draw shot. If your arms happen to be a little shorter than average, you *should* be using slightly longer-than-standard clubs.

The key is whether you can maintain solid clubface-to-ball contact with a 44-inch or even a 45-inch shaft. So, go to the practice tee and start testing.

6. LIE ANGLE

The lie angle is the angle at which the shaft protrudes from the clubhead when it is evenly soled. I use the standard lie angle for the driver, which is 55 degrees.

Lie angle is not really a matter of preference as much as it is one of proper fitting. A correct lie angle is one that allows you to take your normal address position and leaves the club soled nearly dead flat, with just a touch of breathing space under the toe. (The reason for this space is that the shaft actually bows slightly downward in the impact zone, in effect flattening the lie slightly.)

Your Choice

If your arms are longer than average, relative to your height, go with a lie that's flatter than normal. If your arms are short relative to your height, your lie should be a bit more upright than average. Your club pro can take your measurements and determine your correct lie angle.

7. SHAFT MATERIAL

This is another area of club design which has exploded in the past 10 years. While steel still dominates the market, there is a vast array of other materials being put into clubshafts, including graphite, titanium, lightweight steel, boron, and graphite-boron. And different golfers, even top professionals, express different opinions about the playing properties of these various types of shafts. Of course, there are many different flexes in all of these shaft materials, and there is certainly some overlap in the "feels" they will provide.

For most of my career I used dynamic steel shafts, mainly because I hadn't found anything I believed was superior. However, I recently switched to a graphite shaft in the driver. The reason is simply that the graphite shaft supplies a nice, soft feel and a little extra "kick" through impact that gives me confidence and, I believe, a few extra yards of carry on my drives.

Your Choice

You should go with the type of shaft that gives you the best feel and the best response through impact. No clubshaft material has been scientifically proven to be "longer" than the others. If this were the case, believe me, every golfer in the world would be using that clubshaft material.

8. SHAFT FLEX

Here we come to what I believe is the most crucial element in your selection of a driver. If you've got the right shaft flex for your swing characteristics, you're a long way toward having the correct driver.

Today there are many choices available. In steel, for example, the True Temper "Dynamic Gold" system offers five grades of *regular* shafts, five grades of *stiff,* and five grades of *extra-stiff.* Other manufacturers offer similar choice assortments. If your pro shop offers practice clubs with varying shaft stiffnesses, by all means get acquainted with them on the practice tee.

Selecting a driver with a shaft flex suited to your strength and natural swing tendencies is critical to hitting powerful tee shots.

Keep two important points in mind, though:

- The stiffer the shaft, the harder it will be to obtain height and overall carry on your drives.
- Most amateurs try to be "macho" and use shafts that are too stiff for them.

Let me use myself as an example. Until recently I used the stiffest shaft available, a True Temper X500, which is the stiffest shaft in the *extra-stiff* range. Also, the shaft was "tipped" one inch, which makes it substantially stiffer. Maybe I was trying to be "macho" myself: After all, I *am* widely regarded as the longest driver in the world.

However, even I eventually decided that hitting the driver was work with this shaft. When I switched to a graphite shaft made by Aldila, I also went to a stiff rather than an extra-stiff flex. I believe this flex allows me to get the maximum carry on my drives while maintaining reasonable control.

Your Choice

Your shaft flex should be based on the average number of yards you can *carry* the ball with a driver. Don't be too proud to use a flexible shaft. If you do not carry the ball more than 160 yards with a driver under normal conditions, for instance, I believe you should be using a flexible or *ladies'* shaft, whether you are a lady or a man! If your drive carry is over 160 yards but no more than 200 yards, consider shafts within the *regular* range. I don't believe any player who cannot carry the ball 205 yards or more with a driver should be using a stiff shaft. And stay out of the extra-stiff range until you can carry it more than 235 yards. Even if you're ready to enter some long-drive contests, there's no rule that says you must hit *extra-stiffs*.

9. GRIP MATERIAL

The type of grip you can use will fall into one of two major categories—leather or rubber. Within these two choices, there are dozens and dozens of variations.

Leather grips generally are manufactured in long strips that are wrapped around the club's handle area, although one-piece slip-on leather grips are also available. Leather is the choice of a number of professionals because of the wonderful feel and touch it provides. However, leather grips have drawbacks. They must be carefully maintained, because any buildup of dirt and/or perspiration can turn a soft, tacky feel into a hard, slick one. And although treatments of leather grips have improved greatly, they can also lose their tackiness when you play in the rain. Last, leather grips are much more expensive than rubber grips.

Within the rubber category, there is a tremendous variety of patterns and "feels." A number of styles are embedded with a ropy "cord" material. The more cord in the grip, the more secure it may feel, especially in hot weather. However, many golfers believe that these high-cord grips are hard on the hands and reduce that all-important *feel.* On the other end of the spectrum is a variety of much softer, more pliable rubber compounds (with no cord imbedded) which are a great aid to feel for golfers who suffer from arthritis.

I use a fairly soft rubber material, basically because I like the feel and find it secure in all weather conditions.

Your Choice

Grip type is mainly a matter of personal preference. There is no right or wrong material. If you play in a warm climate or if your hands perspire a lot, perhaps a rubber grip with a cord pattern will give you more security. In a cooler climate, a softer rubber may give you better feel. Or leather may be what you really like. Basically, this one is your call.

One last tip: Whatever grip material you use, clean your grips regularly. There will be a dirt buildup after only a couple of rounds; yet some golfers never realize that they're "losing" the club because their grips are slick.

10. GRIP SIZE

Once you've selected your grip material, you must make the important determination of what size grip you should use. Grip size or diameter plays a big role in the degree to which you can release the club through the impact zone. This release, of course, also has a major bearing on your ability to square the clubface and also your clubhead speed at impact.

As a general test for grip size, assume your left-hand grip at its normal point on the handle. The tips of your fingers should barely touch the butt of your palm. If your fingertips dig into the palm, the grip is too thin. If they don't reach your palm, the grip diameter is too large.

Of course, the results of this check depend on your hand size. I happen to have rather large palms but my fingers are short. So, I use a grip that is a shade thinner than standard diameter (1/32 of an inch undersized). This may go against the grain of the macho power hitters who tend to use fat grips; however, I like the feel of the slightly thinner grip and I am positive that it aids my release through impact.

Your Choice

Use the test described as your basic guideline. If your fingers and hands are extremely large, of course, some degree of oversize will be necessary. If anything, though, I

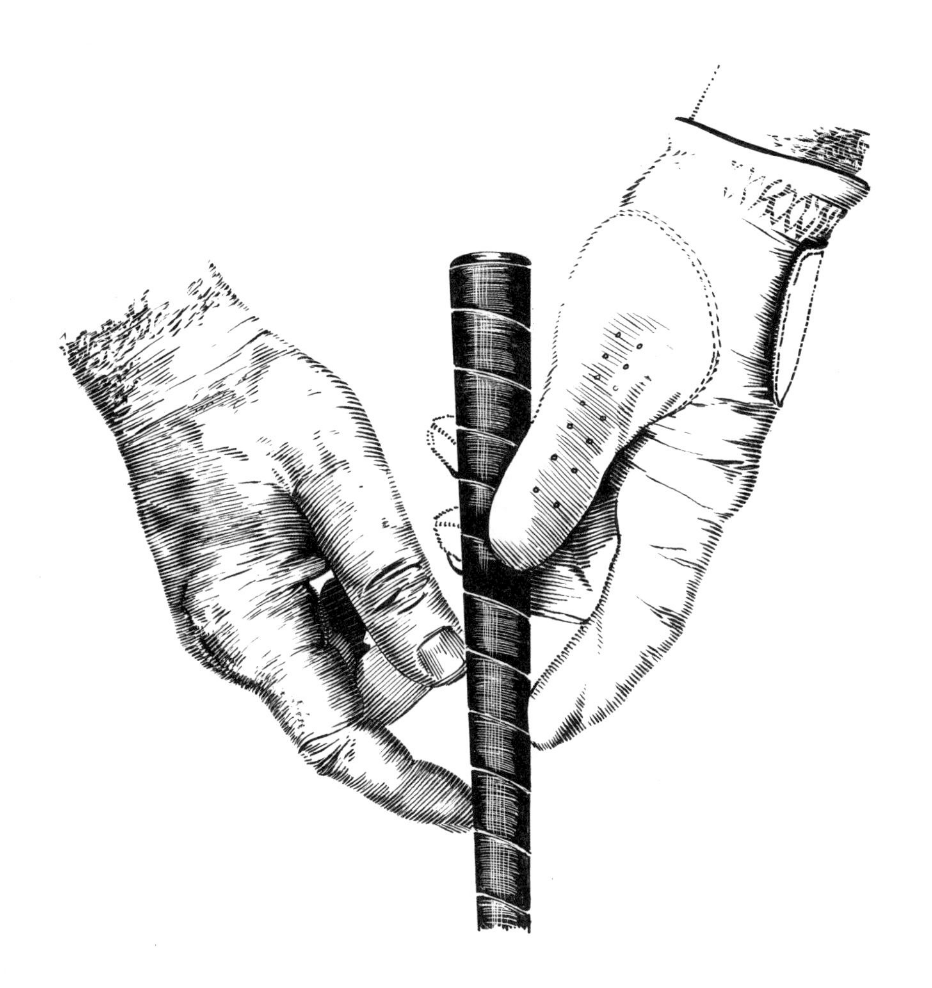

The type of grip you choose should promote good "feel" in your fingers.

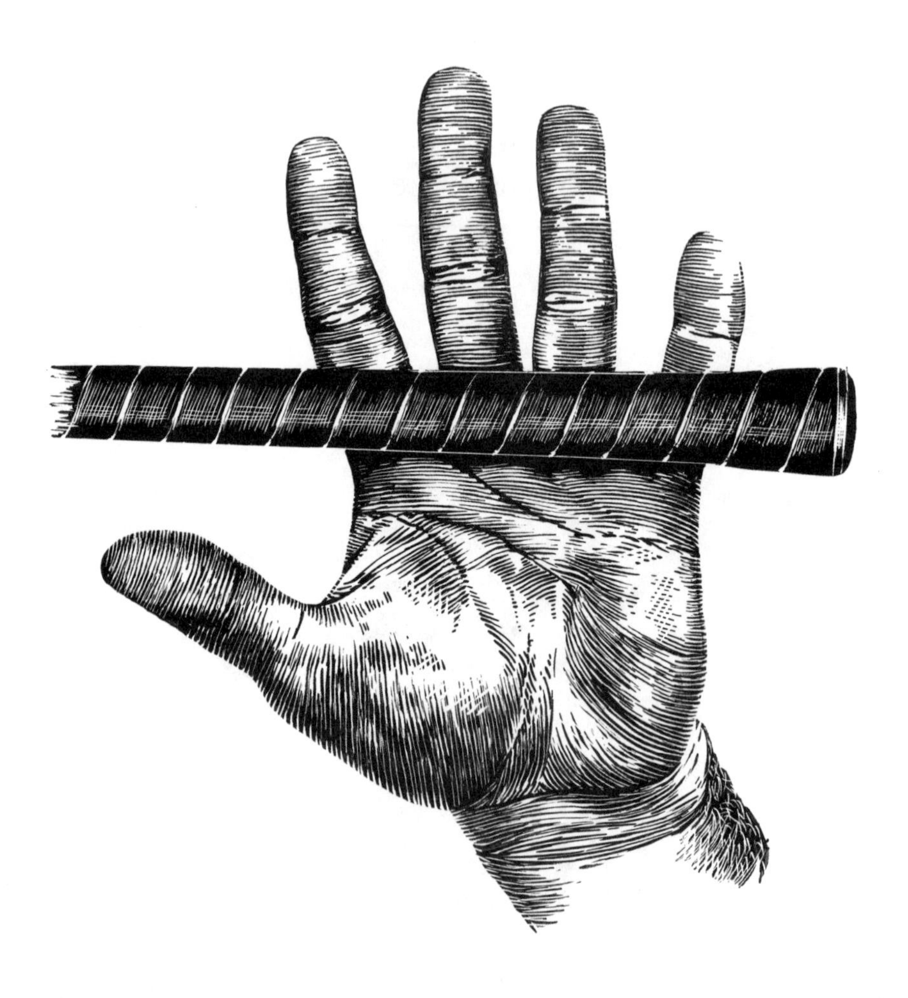

Select a grip that's suited to your hand size.

8

MIND GAMES

You've got to think hard to hit hard

In May 1990, I flew to Tokyo for the first ever Super Long Drive Contest, where I was to match my skills off the tee with the likes of Scott DeCandia, a two-time winner of the National Long Drive Championship, and at that time the current titleholder of that event; Bobby Wilson, the all-time money-winner on the long-drive circuit; Andy Franks, another dual winner of the "Nationals"; and a bunch of other driving brutes, including some local Japanese "ball smashers."

The rules of the contest stipulated that each contestant hit three balls. The one longest drive counted, however, only if it came to rest in the fairway. In other words, a contestant could slug a tee shot a country mile, but if it missed the "short grass," his next longest accurate drive—if it was in the fairway—was the one the judges counted. That's pressure! And on the day of the event, when my name was called to hit, my racing heartbeat and sweating palms signaled that the stakes were high.

As any Sunday golfer will attest, standing on a tee, trying to hit a golf ball long and accurately is a tough enough assignment. But when you consider that I was expected to hit the ball over 300 yards to a target area only 38 yards wide a relatively strong wind was blowing in my face, tall intimidating pines lined the narrow fairway, and a $33,000 first-prize purse was up for grabs, you surely won't be the least bit surprised when I tell you that, when I stood behind the ball to eye up my target, it started to shrink—so much so that the 38-yard-wide patch of fairway I was aiming for looked more like a patchwork quilt!

To make a long story short, on that day in Tokyo, I withstood the "heat" and won! I hit my best drive 318.9 yards, and was also the only player to keep all three tee shots on the fairway. My other two drives flew 315 yards and 309 yards.

I bring up this event, not because of braggadocio, but rather to show and prove to you that even in a high-pressure golf situation, the tables can be turned. I honestly believe that any golfer can perform to a higher standard, provided he physically prepares himself through hard practice on the driving range and mentally prepares himself by learning ways to overcome self-doubt and the fear of success. To quote the great "swinging machine," Ben Hogan: *"The point of golf is to get command of a swing which the more pressure you put on it, the better it works."*

Having already discussed in detail the physical elements and strategies of power golf, this chapter concerns the psychological factors that prepare you for hitting the ball a long distance down the fairway.

CONFIDENCE

Every time I get into a discussion with golfers about the art of long driving, the conversation quickly shifts to the subject of confidence. And, without fail, the same question comes up: Does confidence breed long hitting, or does long hitting breed confidence?

Although this question is as difficult to answer as, "Which comes first, the chicken or the egg?" I still believe that when all the fat is boiled off, confidence, or full trust in one's ability, is what's really important. Why?

I know players with good swings who hit the ball long, but because they lack a true sense of confidence, they are lost when they hit a slump. On the other hand, some unorthodox swingers I know, Scott DeCandia to name just one, perform well under pressure because they are quietly confident.

If I'm giving you the impression that confidence is an innate quality, I don't mean to. Put plain and simply, confidence is a state of mind that results from positive psychological preparation—hard work. This being the case, if you want to hit long drives consistently, in addition to working on your swing, you'll also have to work on getting mentally "pumped up" *before you swing.*

One of the best ways to psyche yourself up with confidence is to vividly picture in your mind's eye a perfectly executed shot, as well as the power swing you must put on the ball. Before you set up, actually *see* the ball's trajectory, flight pattern, and behavior upon landing. Also, *feel* the specific swinging action that you know will turn that fantasy into a reality when it comes time to drive. This preswing routine, or mental rehearsal, not only wipes out any negative thoughts, it disciplines you never to drive until you are fully ready—and *confident.*

Another way of gearing yourself up to hit the ball hard, particularly on an intimidating hole, is to replay in your mind a "top hit" from a past round—a similar drive you successfully planned out in your head and physically played to perfection. This strategy relaxes you; therefore it allows you to plan a shot more carefully and to play it with a high level of confidence.

CONCENTRATION

Concentration, or the ability to give my undivided attention to the tee shot I'm preparing to hit, is one of my biggest assets, and a strength I've nurtured through hitting thousands of practice balls on the driving range.

Practice—hard and honest practice, that is—hones my concentration because it encourages me to:

- Pick out a specific landing area and stare at it for a few seconds.
- See the ball flying off the clubface and splashing into my imaginary "pool."
- Assume a secure setup position that will allow me to swing back correctly and smoothly to the parallel position and deliver the clubface solidly into the ball.
- Focus my eyes intently on the ball.
- Think of *one* specific swing thought to trigger my swing.
- Hit powerfully through the ball.

In saying this, I'm not advocating that you practice until you hit thousands of balls. I am, however, advocating that you take your practice sessions very seriously. Don't just get up and hit ball after ball. Go through a concentrative routine that prepares you for the pressure driving situations you will face on the golf course.

On final tip on concentration: *Don't overdo it.*

When playing an actual round of golf, I suggest that you try to escape into non-golf thoughts between shots. When you walk off the green, look at the blue sky, the ocean, the trees, listen to the birds singing, tell yourself how lucky you are to be on the golf course—take time to "smell the flowers," as the late great golfer Walter Hagen used to say. That way, when you arrive on the next tee, you will feel fresh and ready to let the driver rip.

BRAVERY

Some of my fellow long hitters get pretty philosophical when discussing the attribute of bravery, or fearlessness, or courage—call it what you will—while others claim that a person is born with "heart." Personally, I've seen so many men who are towers of strength in the everyday world shake at the knees when standing over a drive, particularly on the first tee, that I strongly doubt that anyone is truly blessed with bravery at birth.

To novices, it might sound silly for me to mention bravery in a golf book. But I'm sure those of you who have played the game for some years and done battle with the golf course know I'm not being overly dramatic at all.

During a round of golf, we are constantly battling our inner selves, too. Depending on our handicap and the type of round we're playing, we're usually fighting the fear of success or the fear of failure. Good players, or bad players who are having a good round, usually fight the fear of success. Bad players, or good players having a bad day, usually fight the fear of failure.

No matter at what level you play, or how well or poorly you're driving the ball on a particular day, remember one thing: *Bravery is the ability to give each tee shot 100 percent concentration*—to never give up, no matter what. Get in the habit of trying your best on every shot so that when the "heat" is on you'll be groomed for battle—with yourself and with the course.

Every fine player knows that if he keeps his emotions on an even keel, he'll play courageously, even when things don't go precisely as planned. Instead of letting his temper flare and giving up, he stays cool and continues to grind inside his mental cocoon and play at a steady pace. Such a consistently courageous attitude is best nurtured by finding an overall playing speed that allows your adrenaline to flow at the same rate, whether you hit a bad or good drive, or end up scoring a bogie or birdie on a hole. Once you determine the pace of play that's right for you, have the courage to stick to it, no matter how quickly or slowly your partners play.

SELF-DISCIPLINE

Sometimes, when I wake in the morning, I know right away that I'm going to be in for a tough driving day on the course. I feel kind of dull or "cloudy" mentally, my body lacks spring, and for some inexplicable reason, my desire just isn't there. Surely, every golfer feels this way every once in a while.

Granted, the game is so peculiar and hard to predict that a player could actually play his career round on such a sour day. However, this usually does not happen. Normally, if a player feels physically and mentally fatigued, his swing will be out of form and out of time, and his shots will do anything but zoom straight down the middle of the fairway. This is where common sense and discipline come in.

To be a true *golfer,* not just a casual "player," you have to realize that the seemingly simple-looking act of standing to the ball, swinging back and swinging down, comprises numerous complex actions. And for this chain action to work efficiently, a perfect coordination of the mind and the body is necessary. In light of this golf truism, no human being, no matter how talented, can drive the ball well all of the time. Because such variables as strength, coordination, mood, biorhythms, flexibility, timing, tempo, rhythm, mind-set, natural tendencies, and swing thoughts all come into play and determine how well or poorly we swing, good driving days come and go.

I learned long ago, however, from my teacher, Mike Austin, that even on a bad day you can still shoot a pretty good score if you use common sense.

Not being proud is one secret to scoring on those "blue" driving days. If you fade your drives on the practice tee before a round, or on the first couple of holes, don't stubbornly try to make last-minute swing changes in an attempt to hit straight shots. Accept the fact that you just aren't totally yourself on that day, and therefore your swing will not work as efficiently as it does normally.

Instead of trying to amend your fade, allow for its left-to-right flight pattern. Play for it! If you're hooking, apply the same commonsense strategy and aim down the right side of the fairway. If you just can't keep your drives on the fairway at all, play a three-wood off the tee. Because this club is more lofted and shorter than a driver, it is more forgiving on off-center hits and easier to control.

The bottom line: *Be disciplined enough to manage the driving game you bring to the course on a particular day, not the one you had the day before.*

BIOGRAPHY

The Author

John Andrisani is senior editor of instruction at *Golf Magazine* and former assistant editor of the British *Golf Illustrated.*

Andrisani has coauthored three major instruction books with the game's top players: *Learning Golf: The Lyle Way,* with Sandy Lyle; *Natural Golf,* with Seve Ballesteros; *101 Supershots,* with Chi Chi Rodriguez. He is also the coauthor of *The Golf Doctor,* a handy pocket-size booklet that answers just about any question on shotmaking and the game.

A former holder of the American Golf Writers' Championship, Andrisani plays off a 5-handicap at Lake Nona Golf Club, in Orlando, Florida.

The Illustrator

Ken Lewis, who is recognized as one of the world's leading illustrators of the golf swing, has had his unique drawing style compared with the famous artist Anthony Ravielli. He has illustrated numerous books on golf and his work appears regularly in *Golf Magazine* and other worldwide publications.